POEMS OF
THE RING

EZEQUIEL KRATSMAN

Published by: Ezequiel David Publishing
ISBN: 978-1-954314-06-1
Second edition: 2021

To all those who know me, love me, and believe in me.

Prologue

The first time I read a poem dedicated to an athlete was when I was 13 years old. I was reading a book about a basketball player that I have. I don't remember in which chapter the poem was, but it was there. In that moment, I wondered if it was possible dedicating a poem to a famous athlete, even though it didn't rhyme. It was there when I realized it could be done. All you have to do is being creative with the details and you wrote it.

There is here's been hundreds of boxers that had been admired over the years despite how their lives were outside the ring. The fans remember how they used to watch them fight on their televisions or when they went to the coliseums or stadiums to watch them fight. Throughout the years, people keep or kept following boxing and talked about boxers they had seen. They talk about how good they were and what they achieved and in some cases, what else they could have achieved if their careers lasted longer, plus if there were factors that favored them.

They think about how sensational those experiences were. But almost nobody wrote poems dedicated to them at least. In fact, nobody possibly thought about writing one dedicated to a great. And if it happened, barely someone wrote it to someone, but in another language. Because dedicating a poem to a boxer is something not seen.

Have there ever been a collection of poems dedicated only to boxers who made history in that sport? No. It never happened in the long history of literature and in the long history of the sport as well. Many may be wondering: "Who would think about writing a collection of poems dedicated only to boxers? Who?" The answer is: No one thinks about it.

In my life, I watched hundreds and hundreds of boxers fight. I didn't admire some, but I liked their fighting style. I liked every style because every style in the ring entertains the crowd? Why I wrote a collection of poems dedicated to boxers? Let's say it's a challenge I set myself as an author. It's a challenge many maybe can accept and try, but I was willing to try it. Many think doing something like I did in these poems is impossible. If they think this, I can leave you a message: Nothing is impossible in this life. And when I say nothing's impossible, is NOTHING is impossible as long as someone sets his mind to it.

For every boxer I watched, I had a memory about what or how he was. A memory worth describing, depending if someone's interested in hearing. Of course, I appreciate what showed in a ring. That's what I did in every poem I wrote.

In this collection of poems, which gigantic, I wrote poems dedicated to boxers of all weight divisions, from minimumweights to heavyweights. Everyone had qualities in the ring that made them unique. It can be said every poem's an ode. An ode that represents or expresses what that boxer was when he fought. I hope you like it. If some of the mentioned boxers or their relatives, known by their nicknames or how they were known, reads some of the poems and wants to meet me, it'll be an honor. If they or some of their relatives, if they died, want to tell me their anecdotes, I'll be all ears.

Index

Although you did not know when he was going to explode,
you couldn't get careless.
But once he started letting his hands go,
he was simply merciless.
Known as El Inca, as he was known
during the time his career lasted,
he was one of the greatest punchers
there ever was.

A southpaw with dynamite of terror in both hands,
he fought with a tenacious aggressiveness
and once he had chance, he destroyed his opponents
in little pieces with such easiness.
During his career, he crushed opponents in a matter
of seconds without pity and without elegance.
He won all his pro fights;
none of them went the distance.

During his career, he won championships
as a super featherweight and as lightweight,
proving he was one of the most excited
fighters to watch in his day.
It's sad his life ended abruptly,
leaving an unfinished legacy in the boxing world.
His career ended with a big what if for those fans
who watched him fight and love the sport.

Tribute to Edwin Valero

Exciting the crowd with his power
and aggressive style was the best thing he could do.
Once the fight was on, he would fight
with the intention of demolishing you.
His punches were so powerful
and fought with relentlessness
if an opponent lasted more than a one round,
it was miraculous success.

One of the best heavyweights of all-times,
he never took a step back once he heard the bell sound.
He would keep going until he knocked you down
and watched the referee reach the ten-count.
With his noticed and unmeasurable ferocity,
he could attack the mid-section
or knock someone out with good punches to the jaw,
becoming at his time the biggest fight attraction.

That's why he was the Manassa Mauler.
He made every opponent look fragile.
His aggressive style, besides making an attraction,
helped him the world heavyweight title.
He won the world heavyweight championship,
destroying a man who was twice his size.
One of the best boxers of all times,
he left the crowd mesmerized.

Tribute Jack Dempsey

The Korean Hawk   May 2019

Almost no one in the ring
could match his resistance.
His fighting style was accepted
even if his fights went the distance.
He had very good quickness and strength
in both hands for a light flyweight.
The Korean Hawk had a will of rock
nobody could underestimate in any way.

A Korean version of The Hawk from the United States,
he was one of most exiting fighters in the game.
The crowd was never disappointed
because his fights could always entertain.
He had more than a dozen successful title defenses,
being of those champions you can rarely find.
He showed his talent in a glorious reign
where he truly shined.

One of the most prestigious talents
in the history of South Korea,
he also one of the best light flyweights
and one of the best fighters of his era.
He was one of the best Asians boxers ever.
He left thousands and thousands of fans with a memory
of one of the best fighters in the lighter weight divisions
and one of the best boxers in history.

Tribute to Jung-Koo Chang

He was a known as a great gentleman
coming out of Managua.
He's without a doubt the best boxer
in the history of Nicaragua.
One of the most elegant champions in the ring
and one of the best there ever was.
He was a champion with a great fighting style
and a champion with class.

With his bony elbows and long, skinny arms,
his defense looks like a shell.
Yet, he could avoid punches
and defend himself very well.
A fighter with power and finesse,
He threw great combinations.
His punches to the body and the head were paralyzing
and he was a great figure in the lighter divisions.

Watching him fight was an honor.
He was a tall man with lanky physique,
but everything he fought a in ring,
he showed power and tremendous technique.
He won titles in the featherweight, super featherweight,
and in the lightweight divisions in his time of glory.
Known as the Explosive Thin Man, this Nicaraguan legend
was one of the best fighters in boxing history.

Tribute to Alexis Argüello

Known as The Hawk, his fights
were talked about even in the streets.
He was a fighter opponents had
issues dealing with.
Almost none of his fights
lasted until the final round, meaning
his opponent always ended in the ground.

He pointed at his opponent like an arrow
with his right hand
and then, prepared to fight,
which was expected by every fan.
He was a fighting machine
threw punches tirelessly from any angle.
His punching power was tremendous
and his stamina was remarkable.

He could take punches and give them too,
and if he got down, it angered him more.
He would get up, and his tireless attack continued.
He was simply one of the best super lightweights in the sport.
The Hawk was a human windmill who dominated
his opponents in his time of glory.
A great world super lightweight champion,
he was one of the best boxers in history.

Tribute to Aaron Pryor

When it came to showing toughness,
he was an undisputed master.
He fought with the mentality of a sinister man,
which was one of his qualities as a fighter.
He was a machismo symbol;
he had a very solid jaw.
This Panamanian legend's hands
could do more damage than a chainsaw.

He punched hard with both fists
and never showed his opponents any compassion.
He fought with the same ferocity and mercilessness
as moved up in weight division.
He won championships as a lightweight, welterweight,
super welterweight, and as a middleweight.
He won more than 100 fights, becoming
one of the few boxers to do so in his day.

Known as the "Hands of Stone",
he was one of the most recognized athletes in the world.
He became a myth in boxing and was
the greatest modern warrior in the sport.
He was a guy who had the complete package
and knew how to get the job done,
and was one of the best boxers of all times.
That was the legend known as the Hands of Stone.

Tribute to Roberto Durán

The Pacman doesn't stop attacking
and throwing punches once the round begins.
His spirit and mind say: "Keep attacking",
until the round ends.
In a very hard sport, where every fighter
is required to have a good defense,
in his case, his best defense
is his incredible offense.

An incredibly fast individual,
his fists are quicker than lighting.
The combinations from unpredictable angles
are simple dazzling.
His punches can cause damage anywhere
and he throws quick punches his opponents can't see.
He fights with such intensity it's something
fans have to see.

A world champion in multiple divisions,
he enters the ring to get the job done.
This Filipino legend throws combinations
faster than a machine gun.
A famous figure worldwide, those fans who watched
this incredible southpaw boxer will have a memory
of one of the greatest Asian boxers ever
and one of the best in history.

Tribute to Manny Pacquiao

Known as "The Brown Bomber",
outside the ring, he was a quiet man,
but inside a ring,
he could knock you out with either hand.
He was one of those guys that
didn't talk a lot in a press conference.
he just let his fists do the talking
and most of his opponents didn't last the distance.

His punches were so and powerful
that could destroy guys
that only were more experienced,
but were also bigger in size.
He faced the toughest lions in the heavyweight division,
and beat them convincingly.
With great accuracy and speed, he could knockdown
opponents and knock them out with great facility.

After winning the world heavyweight championship,
he defended it twenty-five times in his reign,
and hold it longer than any other fighter in his division,
becoming one of the best heavyweights in the game.
An idol and icon that was idolized by millions,
he left millions of fans with a wonderful memory
of one of the best heavyweights ever,
and one of the best fighters in boxing history.

Tribute to Joe Louis

Known as "The Durable Dane", he was one
of those guys that dominated the rough-and-tumble world.
This great lightweight was one of the toughest
and most durable guys in the history of the sport.
In this day, he took punishment that in the modern day,
it would be considered brutal,
but when he fought,
it seemed he thought it was normal.

In a time where boxers dared to fight
anybody, anytime, and anywhere,
he made every fight look like a war and was willing
to take everything his opponent had to offer.
He would take his opponents' best punches
to be able to land many of his own.
At the end of the fight, the opponents ended
discouraged and knocked down.

He was a guy who hit hard with both hands
and even amazed fans who seated at ringside.
He could fight dozens of rounds taking
and giving punishment every fight.
He won the world lightweight championship
in a career where he shined.
He was one of the greatest lightweights ever
and one of the greatest fighters in history.

Tribute to Battling Nelson

One of the best of his day,
known as "The Canastota Onion Farmer",
Everyone in his era enjoyed watching
the fights of this great fighter.
He was one of those guys
who could really take it.
Every time he entered the ring,
he was always ready to bring it.

He was of those fighters who could
bring a lot of excitement every night.
He showed a soul of steel
and an incredible desire to win every fight.
He could take his opponents' punches
due to his unbreakable granite chin.
He was of those courageous warriors
fans enjoyed seeing in a boxing ring.

You could hit him with a plank and yet,
there was no way you knock him down.
He could out-fight, out-war, and out-punch you
until sending you to the ground.
He won the world welterweight and middleweight titles
in a career where he truly shined.
He was one of most courageous and determined boxers
and one of the best of all times.

Tribute to Carmen Basilio

Finito   May 2019

He left the world mesmerized
despite being a minimumweight.
He was one of the finest boxers
and ring technicians of his day.
This legend known as Finito
had a very slender physique,
but he could hit really hard
and had an exquisite technique.

One of the best fighters in the history of México,
this phenomenal little man
showed his great skills in places like
South Korea, Japan, and Thailand.
A world champion in two divisions, he had
twenty-two title defenses as minimumweight,
then he moved up in weight
and became a world champion as a light flyweight.

One of the greatest little men ever,
he had speed, technique, effectiveness,
and other attributes he showed
in his era of greatness.
One of the few boxers to retire undefeated,
left many fans with a great memory
of the best minimumweight of all times
and one of the best boxers in history.

Tribute to Ricardo López

He was an excellent counterpuncher
and a really gifted one.
Known as "Dinamita", this Mexican legend
always knew how to get the job done.
He was a boxer with great speed
and could throw very long combinations.
Nobody could block them easily
and was as good as a mathematician solving equations.

Everybody remembers his great battles
with the Filipino star named Pacman,
a rivalry of four fights that left a memory
in the heart of every fan.
Despite being knocked down several times,
he gave a great fight to overcome his adversary.
However, the judges didn't see him winning
the first three fights of the rivalry.

Then, he gave the Filipino cyclone a knockout for the ages
in a historic fourth fight.
Many people, including his opponent, left the arena
with a memory of that great night.
He gave a beautiful boxing clinic in the ring
every time he shined.
He was one of Mexico's greatest fighters ever
and one of the best of all times.

Tribute to Juan Manuel Márquez

He was really young when he started
fighting as a professional.
But he showed his quality
in the ring was beyond sensational.
In an age where most young people
are in high school or at the university,
he was showing he was an extraordinary fighter,
facing the best and taking them to school convincingly.

He showed incredible maturity at a young age.
The Radar was someone who rarely trained.
Yet, he made his fights
look like a chess game.
When he was against the ropes,
he made you think you could finish him in the ring.
But he could dodge your lefts and rights
without any problem and could win.

The Radar will be remembered as one
of the greatest defensive masters in history,
one who defended himself and attacked accurately
and shined in his time of glory.
He will also be remembered for his flaw of not training,
a quality that led him to get triumphs amazingly,
but in the end, it declined his legendary greatness
and costed him dearly.

Tribute to Wilfred Benítez

One of the best featherweights
and of Mexico's best fighters there ever was.
Fans enjoyed watching this great nicknamed Chava,
one who proved he improved as years passed.
He had a gigantic jaw and the look
of a choir kid.
But in the ring, he was a boxer
opponent always struggled with.

He was an excellent counterpuncher;
he combined his counterattacks with quickness.
He landed really powerful punches
that did not lose their aggressiveness.
His counterpunching was his best weapon,
a weapon no one could underestimate.
He was one of the best fighters
and counterpunchers of his day.

He's remembered for his memorable fight
against Bazooka, the Puerto Rican legend,
who underestimated him constantly,
but splashed him like leech at the end.
He never lost a title defense, and was
a wonderful boxer to watch in his prime.
He was one of Mexico's best fighters
and one of the best fighters of all times.

Tribute to Salvador Sánchez

One of Argentina's all-time greats,
he was a little giant full of tenacity.
He was an impressive fighter
who impressed any type of adversity.
Like in many cases,
he was the smaller guy.
But he always showed why
he was a real champion every night.

Falucho had a seasoned style,
where he avoided his opponents' hands
with good head movement and unloaded a non-stop
attack the neutralized his rivals' fight plans.
It was really hard for his rivals
to stop him because once he decided
which punches to throw and land, he
could knock them down in a fight.

A real fighter and traveler who won
world championships as a flyweight and a super flyweight,
he fought in many foreign places, proving he would fight
anywhere, anytime, and any day.
A two-division champion who earned the respect
and admiration of million who watched in his prime,
this Argentinian legend was one of the greatest little men
and one of the best boxers of all times.

Tribute to Santos Benigno Laciar

El Leopardo de Morón   May 2019

Known as El Leopardo de Morón,
or the Leopard of Morón,
he was another of Argentina's greats
and could out-battle you round after round.
He wasn't a great technical boxer,
but could battle anyone like he was in a war.
He was a bull that gave his rival no room
to do his fight plan, and stopping him was hard.

Everyone remembers his historic fight
in the South African nation,
where he had a head clash and got cut badly,
but kept fighting with an unmeasurable determination.
He attacked like a mad fiery,
knocking his opponent down
and beating him by a dramatic knockout
in the last seconds of the fifteenth and final round.

He was a great battler in the ring
who feared no man.
He fought with a determination mixed with ferocity
until the end.
This legend known as "El Leopardo de Morón",
who fought in the light heavyweight division,
was one of the greatest fighters ever
and one of the best of his generation.

Tribute to Víctor Galíndez

He was your worst nightmare
once you were in the ring.
He could make you leave the arena in a stretcher after
he landed one punch on you with the fury he had within.
Anyone who watched Iron Mike
remembers his brutal nature.
His fists, more solid than a sledgehammer,
could inflict a pain nobody could endure.

In just a fraction of a second, Iron Mike
he could knock someone down.
His attacks were so lethal and powerful
half of his opponents didn't last the first round.
He had a great muscled physique, tremendous defense,
great in-fighting, impressive hand speed,
incredible reflexes, and natural punching power,
making him a fighter who was extremely hard to deal with.

He became the youngest world heavyweight champion ever
and one of the most feared in the game.
Then, he suffered his first loss and lost his title in Japan,
and since then, things were never the same.
Although his greatness became a memory,
he was great to watch in his prime.
He was one of the greatest punchers, one of boxing's best
heavyweights and one of the best of all times.

Tribute to Mike Tyson

The Golden Boy

One of the most exciting fighters ever,
he won an Olympic gold medal
and then, he shined as a pro.
Known as the Golden Boy, he was sensational.
He had a great left look
developed since his amateur days.
He had great speed, threw fast combinations;
he could amaze in many ways.

With the help of his qualities,
he shined in his career as a professional.
He became an attraction, an idol,
and his ring wins were sensational.
He won world championship
from super featherweight to middleweight.
That's six weight divisions, making him one
of the most accomplished fighters of his day.

This great American idol gave many boxing fans
great memories and joy.
Many had to say at some point of their lives:
"When I grow up, I want to be like the Golden Boy".

Tribute to Oscar De La Hoya

He was another admired world champion
in the featherweight division.
On second, you thought he was finished,
the next one, he sent you to your destruction.
His fights could never disappoint
a boxing fan.
He out-punched his opponent, made him
feel his power in either hand.

He had almost all his wins by knockout;
most of his opponent didn't last the scheduled rounds.
Known as Little Red, he made his opponent
suffer hard knockdowns.
He easily destroyed every fighter that
challenged him during his reign.
His devastating fist made him one
of the biggest punchers in the game.

Little Red was always willing to battle.
He was a little man, but he was powerful.
His wins and fights were
always wonderful.
Those who watched him fight
were left with a great memory
of one of the greatest punchers
and one of the best boxers in history.

Tribute to Danny López

A great Cuban legend who
threw the bolo punch with precision.
He was a spectacular fighter who shined
in the era of television.
He earned the hearts of millions
of boxing admirers
who watched him on their television
facing the best fighters.

Known as The Cuban Hawk, he was one
of the greatest champions in the welterweight division
and one of the greatest coming out of Cuba.
His fights entertained a generation.
During his long career,
he was never knocked out in the ring.
He always gave fans their money's worth,
whenever he got a loss or a win.

Those fans who watched the Cuban Hawk
in those times left the arena with a memory
of one of the best Cuban boxers
and one of the greatest in history.

Tribute to Kid Gavilan

Sugar Ray (The Original)   May 2019

There won't be another like the original Sugar Ray.
He could make a step back
and at the same time, knock you out with one punch.
He was the best there ever was.
He was famous worldwide.
His skills were so superior
that in his prime, he made every opponent
look simply inferior.

After an unbeaten amateur career,
he turned professional,
where he didn't lose until his forty-first pro bout.
After that bout, he looked infinitely sensational.
His left hand was always in pure movement.
He overcame everybody with his speed.
He threw punches in combinations
that the opponents could not see.

He won the world welterweight championship one
and hold the world middleweight title on five occasions.
He gave boxing clinics to the best boxing offered
and impacted many generations.
In his farewell night, at the Mecca of boxing, he received
a trophy that said: "The best fighter in the world".
This legend, that was poetry in motion, was the best
pound-per-pound boxer in the history of the sport.

Tribute to Sugar Ray Robinson

For his small island, it was an honor
watching him fight every round.
He made thousands of his countrymen happy
when he sent his opponents to the ground.
He was some Muhammad Ali to his island
and was always like that.
Since his fame increased, he became one
of Puerto Rico's most admired athletes there ever was.

Known as Tito, this fighter could knock anyone out
with one punch thrown by either hand.
His fists were so and so powerful
he could drop any man.
He was a great champion
in his three reigns.
He destroyed his opponents to become
one of the most lethal punchers in the game.

Thousands of his compatriots enjoyed
chanting: "Tito! Tito!", when he had a fight.
It became a myth every time he fought,
making the event an electrifying night.
A gentleman and a likable personality,
Tito left the fans with a wonderful memory
of one of boxing's greatest punchers, one of the
most beloved champions, and one of the best fighters in history.

Tribute to Felix "Tito" Trinidad

A phenomenon with superlative level
that came from Quilmes.
He was one of the great talents
boxing the fans had the pleasure to witness.
His elusive style with his hands down
attracted millions of fans.
A technical fighter with a warrior's mentality,
he could hit and had very quick hands.

A very gifted southpaw who fought everywhere,
he didn't get some decisions
he deserved and many fans know it.
However, his style impressed many generations.
People remember his second fight with The Punisher,
when he gave one of the best knockouts of all times.
He won the world super welterweight and middleweight
titles when he truly shined.

Known as Maravilla, a Spanish world
that means Marvelous.
He had incredible reflexes and a brilliant mind.
The boxing lessons he gave were fabulous.
An astute boxer who amazed the crowd,
he showed greatness in his time of glory,
becoming one of the most exciting fighters
and one of Argentina's greatest in history.

Tribute to Sergio Martínez

Only three man were very fortunate
to last the bout's final round.
Normally, other opponents who felt
his powerful punches were easily knocked down.
He landed destructive punches
wherever it was possible.
Taking his punches in the ring
was almost impossible.

Known as "Bazooka", he unloaded
an unstoppable ammunition at his rival's humanity,
knocking them out and leaving them
on the canvas in any occasion.
Although he won world titles in the featherweight
and the super featherweight divisions,
his time as a super bantamweight world champion
was the best of any fighter of his generation.

He made seventeen successful defenses
during his reign as a super bantamweight,
all of them knockout, ending his challengers
like a lion who finished his prey.
A knock-out artist, who destroyed his rivals
like a puma, he was great to watch in his prime.
He was the best super bantamweights ever
and one of the best boxers of all times.

Tribute to Wilfredo Gómez

It was worth seeing
this great light heavyweight.
He was one of the best masterful
technicians of his day.
Known as "The Phantom of Philly",
he had to be admired for his ability.
He was a boxer with marvelous ring generalship
and with amazing agility.

He had a very good defensive tactic,
but most importantly, an incredible left.
It was that great left hand to controlled the distance
and gave boxing lessons to even the best.
He didn't have great punching power,
but he showed splendid technique in the ring,
reminding boxing fans you don't necessarily
need only power to win.

One of the most amazing technicians
and boxing masters of his generation,
he gave boxing clinics to the best
in the light heavyweight and heavyweight division.
A great world light heavyweight champion
who could make any opponent look silly,
and one of the best boxers of all times;
that's the legacy of The Phantom of Philly.

Tribute to Tommy Loughran

Known as "Escopeta", or Shotgun,
he was probably the best middleweight in history.
He made millions of Argentinians happy
when he had his time of glory.
Nobody was able to beat him
when he was a world champion.
He was even admired in Europe, when he destroyed
his opponents with more barbarism than a lion.

He was a great of champion,
an idol of matinee.
He was one of the great champions
who came from Santa Fe.
He fought with great logic, and intelligence,
and an economic aggressiveness.
He beat every opponent as a world middleweight champion
in his moment of greatness.

He lost three of his first twenty fights,
but after that, he never lost again.
He had fourteen successful title defenses
in his middleweight reign.
He was one of the most popular fighters of his era,
those watched him ended or have a memory
of the one considered by many the best
Argentinian boxer ever and one of the best in history.

Tribute to Carlos Monzón

Iron Boy   May 2019

Every time he stepped on a ring,
he was a bullfighter.
He was always the smaller man, but his ring
generalship could frustrate any fighter.
During his long reign
in the minimumweight division,
he showed he was one of most
elegant and purest boxers of his generation.

The way he moved around the ring and dodged
hundreds of punches was art.
Known as "Iron Boy", hitting him
effectively was extremely hard.
Even in his light flyweight reign, he showed
he was one of the most masterful boxers in recent memory.
He was one of Puerto Rico's best boxers and one
of the best little men in history.

Tribute to Iván Calderón

Known as the Galveston Giant, he
was great heavyweight.
In and out of the ring, he was
the most hated man of his day.
He was a heavyweight, but he moved
in the ring like a cat,
could easily avoid punches and no one
knew how to deal with something like that.

He hit with punches as quick as a bullet,
he could fight, and fended himself with elegance.
He also used to smile at his opponents
and show arrogance.
He became the first black
world heavyweight champion in history
in a hard time for society.
He had a long reign of glory.

When he lost the title in Cuba,
his heavyweight came to an end.
A high-caliber fighter of his day,
he was one of the most recognized men.
He was one of those guys who gave a good effort
and left an impression in the sporting world.
He was one of the best heavyweights ever and one
of the best boxers in the history of the sport.

Tribute to Jack Johnson

La Locomotora   May 2019

Known as "La Locomotora", or The
Locomotive when he shined,
this man was also one of the best
Argentinian fighters of all times.
He was another figure who reigned
as a middleweight.
He was one of the hardest hitters and one
of the toughest guys in the game.

Who doesn't remember La Locomotora?
He got tough when he really had to.
He didn't have great technique, but he could hit
and knock you out when wanted to.
You couldn't get careless with him.
Everyone remembers that night
in Mexico, where was losing, and with a great left hook,
beat his opponent in an historic fight.

He won that historic bout by knockout
in what became of boxing a great end of the year.
It was probably the best definition, the biggest
and most remembered win of his career.
Anyone who watched La Locomotora
left the arena with a memory
one of the best Argentinian fighters ever
and one of the greatest hitters in history.

Tribute to Jorge Fernando Castro

The Fierce Eagle   May 2019
(Kanmuriwashi)

He had a short career
as a professional.
But during that time,
he proved he was sensational.

One of Asia's greatest champions,
every he stepped on a ring, this great Japanese
showed great offense and stamina,
and demolished his opponent with ease.

He had a very good reign
as a light flyweight
and proved he was one
of the best Japanese boxers of his day.

Known as the Fierce Eagle,
when he was a champion, he shined.
He was one of Japan's best boxers
and one of the best light flyweights of all times.

Tribute to Yoko Gushiken

The Brockton Blockbuster   May 2019

Known as "The Brockton Blockbuster",
he was very small for a heavyweight,
but he indestructible stamina, and was
one of the greatest punchers in history and of his day.
He had a solid and granite jaw
and was a swarmer in the ring.
He was a perfect example of showing desire
and doing anything to win.

He had a short reach and short arms,
but his hands were more solid than a tank,
and could send anyone to the ground
with his devastating and thunderous right hand.
He applied constant pressure every split second
until the round came to an end.
He would be on you again
once the next round would began.

He could take incredible punishment,
and yet he moved forward like a machine.
He was of those great warriors that gave it
all every time he was in the ring.
He's the only world heavyweight champion
to retire undefeated during his time of glory.
He was one of the best heavyweights, greatest punchers,
and one of the best boxers in history.

Tribute to Rocky Marciano

El Zurdo   May 2019
(The left-handed)

Another of Argentina's great champions,
he was a great junior middleweight.
Another champion coming out of Santa Fe,
he was one of the great hitters of his day.
He was a southpaw who could demolish
and knock an opponent down with his left hand.
He had punching power with both hands,
but his left hand could mesmerize any fan.

As a world light middleweight champion,
he had a long reign,
having twelve successful title defenses,
being one of the great champions in the game.
Known as "El Zurdo", or The Left-handed,
he was admired by millions of Argentinians.
Like many champions, his fighting style
was watched by thousands of fans.

One of the greatest Argentinian fighters ever,
even though he kept fighting when he was past his prime,
he was one of the great light middleweights
and was worth watching when he had his time.

Tribute to Julio César Vásquez

Zurdo   May 2019
(Left-handed)

Another of Argentina's greats
who never got a shot at the middleweight title.
He deserves more credit than what he gets
because he was remarkable.
He was a left-handed who fought
at the orthodox stance.
Yet, his opponents felt his punching power
and they didn't go the distance.

He was a fighter who had great ability
with both hands.
His knockout wins over the years
impressed many fans.
His opponents ended like a prey
hunted by a lion.
He will be remembered as a great fighter
who ended his career as a non-champion.

He faces the best contenders in the division
and beat them at their best.
During his career, he showed
he had potential for greatness.
He never had a chance for the middleweight title
he deserved; he could've had more glory.
He was one of the best non-champions
and one of the greatest punchers in boxing history.

Tribute to Eduardo Lausse

Known as "The Bronx Bull", he
had one of the best chins in the world.
He was also one of the toughest competitors
in the long history of the sport.
He gave fans their money's worth
and was a tough fighter to deal with.
He fought with a volcanic rage
and had the style of a street kid.

His jaw was so solid that nobody
could knock him down even if he had the chance.
He had small hands and great body attack.
Most of his fights went the distance.
Even the best pound-per-pound
fighter of all times
was unable to send him to the canvas
in the great rivalry they had in their prime.

This middleweight with the body of a light heavyweight
fought like a volcano ready to get an eruption.
He absorbed an incredible amount of punishment
to attack his rival's anatomy with no compassion.
The Bronx Bull will be remembered as one of the
toughest fighters with gloves in his time of glory.
He was one of the best middleweights ever
and one of the best boxers in history.

Tribute to Jake LaMotta

Known as "El Púas", he's in the long list
of boxing's great little men,
but he had great punching power in both fists,
especially in his left hand.

His left hook was thrown and landed
with more power than a cannonball
that was just fired
and landed on a wall.

Some remember the version of El Púas
who fought as a featherweight
when he became a world champion.
He was at his best as a bantamweight.

This Mexican legend shined better as a bantamweight
where he won his first world championship
and had that potent left hook that left opponent
on the canvas like a sunk ship.

A powerful puncher with explosiveness,
those who watched him fight have a great memory
of one of Mexico's greatest boxers
and one of the greatest fighters in boxing history.

Tribute to Rubén Olivares

He was known as J.C.,
among other nicknames.
He was the greatest Mexican boxer
in the history of the game.
All his Mexican compatriots supported him
every time he entered the ring.
He was one of the greatest modern warriors.
He always prepared to win.

He was a legend whose fighting style
impacted a great generation.
He was always after his opponent,
going forward with tireless aggression.
With a good bending, technique, and power,
he was willing to take a punch to land one.
Once the opponent felt his punches in the body
or in the jaw, he was gone.

He didn't lose for almost a decade and a half.
He won championship in three weight divisions:
super featherweight, lightweight, and super lightweight.
He was admired by millions.
He had many title defenses and those fans that came
to the fights with the Mexican flag have a great memory
of the greatest Mexican fighter ever
and one of the best boxers in history.

Tribute to Julio César Chávez

The Old Mongoose

May 2019

He was dodged a lot of times during his long career,
but he kept showing his ring generalship,
fighting, and battling until he won
the world light heavyweight championship.
He won the world champion at an age
where fighters are no longer in their prime.
But he still managed to prove he was one
of the best light heavyweights of all times.

He kept fighting and beating everyone
despite getting old,
earning a reputation as an experienced fighter
and one of the greatest fighters in the world.
Known as "The Old Mongoose", he fought
the best contenders and opponents he could face.
He fought them and beat them regardless
of age, experience, and race.

With great punching power in both hands,
intelligence and armadillo defense,
he beat the best whether he won by knockout
or the other guys lasted the distance.
One of the greatest light heavyweights ever,
he had many moments of glory.
A great puncher he scored more knockouts
than any other boxer in history.

A fighter who traveled millions of miles
and fought every opponent cleverly.
He had a long reign as world champion
and landed powerful punches effectively.

He fought in many places and whenever he won, lost,
or had a draw, he never made an excuse.
One of the best boxers ever; that was this legend
nicknamed The Old Mongoose.

Tribute to Archie Moore

Known was "Mantequilla" in his career,
he was one of the best of his generation.
Originally from Cuba, he then moved to Mexico,
a country with a rich boxing tradition.
He had a very good fighting style
with a very decent technique.
Besides having punching power in both hands,
he was also smooth and slick.

Nobody forgets the legend of Mantequilla
and his welterweight championship reign
where he beat his opponents clearly and was
one of the best boxer-punchers in the game.
He had great ability in the ring
mixed with tremendous tenacity.
The only issue was his sensitive eyebrows
that made him get cut easily.

He had a great left hand he threw
great combinations with fluidly.
He showed fluency of many dimensions
and that's something you don't see constantly.
He had two reigns as a welterweight;
and a great career where he shined.
He was one of the best welterweights ever
and one of the best boxers of all times.

Tribute to José Nápoles

The Boilermaker   May 2019

Like many fighters in the sport,
he had a short career as a professional.
But that enough for him to earn
admirers because he was sensational.
He had enough bouts to achieve
success in the sport
and win the world heavyweight championship,
the biggest title in the sport.

Known as "The Boilermaker", he had his left arm extended
and the body a little crouched down to the right,
a position that made him unpredictable
and worked for him every fight.
He was a puncher who could take a punch
and had an incredible strength.
He had enough power to finish
and destroy any man.

He was one of the biggest hitters and
beat some of the best fighters in the game.
He could've stay undefeated,
but came out of retirement to fight once again.
He fought the legend nicknamed "The Galveston Giant".
He fought that legend when he was past his prime
and lost, a sad ending to the career of the great considered
by many one of the best fighters of all times.

Tribute to James J. Jeffries

Nobody who watched him can forget him.
He was a figure anyone could idolize.
Although he didn't knock guys out, his ability
to defend himself left everyone mesmerized.
He didn't have a relentless attack, but his ability
to dodge punches was beyond remarkable.
No wonder this legend from Mendoza, Argentina
was known as "The Untouchable".

His defensive skills in the ring
were something almost impossible to deal with.
It was possible he couldn't knock you out,
but he could spend rounds without getting hit.
No other stylist could deal
with his infinitely wonderful ring generalship.
His incredible technique and defense led him
to the world super lightweight championship.

This Argentinian legend was simply elegant,
if you threw two hundred punches, he dodged them easily.
He had unmatchable reflexes, he was a star
that could avoid punishment fluidly.
He was wonderful boxer to watch
when he had his time of glory.
He was one of the best defensive masters ever
and one of the best boxers in boxing history.

Tribute to Nicolino Locche

Known as "El Leon Mendocino", or the Lion
of Mendoza; another Argentinian great.
He was a very small man, but
was a really hard hitter for a flyweight.
Every time he stepped on a ring,
he was the ring with a smaller size,
but with his ferocity and punching power,
he could destroy other guys.

He pressured his opponents,
putting them through a nightmare.
With his hitting power, he
could hurt them anywhere.
A pioneer in Argentinian sport,
his ring career was remarkable.
He became the first Argentinian boxer
to win a world title.

A world flyweight champion, he excelled
in the ring despite his small frame.
His tenacious and tremendous attack
made him have a great flyweight reign.
One of the smallest champions of all times,
he gave Argentina a lot of glory.
He was one of the greatest flyweights
and one of the best boxers in history.

Tribute to Pascual Pérez

El Alacrán   May 2019

Known as "El Alacrán", or "The Scorpion",
he had a dominant reign as a featherweight.
This all-time great from Panama
was one of the best fighters of his day.
He made nineteen successful title defenses
as the featherweight champion of the world.
El Alacrán fought some
of the best fighters in the sport.

His performance improved a lot
as rounds passed.
He often showed tactics that are not clean,
but still proved he was one of the best there ever was.
A guy with power, heart, and aggressiveness,
he was great to watch in his prime.
This Panamanian legend was one of the best featherweights
and one of the best boxers od all times.

Tribute to Eusebio Pedroza

El Toro   May 2019

Known as "El Toro", and another nickname,
he had the height of a lightweight,
but he had the body and physical
aspect of a cruiserweight.

He imposed his heart in the ring
to fight other guys.
He dared to fight the best opponents
available, regardless of size.

His toughness and heart led him
to the cruiserweight championship of the world.
One of Argentina's great champions,
he did great fights in the sport.

Tribute to Marcelo Domínguez

He was the boss of his own performance
after, during, and after a fight.
He backed up everything he said
during a fight night.
Whatever he was to going to say,
he was going to back it up in every moment.
Even when he fought in a ring,
it was pure entertainment.

Something amazing about him
is he could fulfill his prediction.
He was like a prophet who predicted how the fight
would end, and kept up his word with precision.
He was a boxer worth seeing.
He had the body of a heavyweight
and the speed and agility
of a lightweight.

He had his hands down and yet,
the opponents couldn't hit him
because he had great reflexes and was faster than fast.
He could finish a fight with his face clean.
Known as "The Greatest",
not only he was known for his physique,
but also for his mental brilliance
and impressive technique.

In his first title shot and in the Rumble in the Jungle,
people thought he had no chance,
but he proved them wrong
by giving an incredible performance.
He was one of the greatest icons
and most globally recognized athletes in the sport.

Watched and idolized by millions, he had three reigns
as the heavyweight champion of the world.

His legacy had impacted millions of people,
including hundreds of boxers.
He truly was the Greatest,
in the eyes of millions of his followers.

Tribute to Muhammad Ali

He's also part of the list
of Argentina's great champions in the sport.
He was also an Argentinian idol
who won the flyweight championship of the world.

Known as Roquiño, he was a southpaw
who could really fight.
He had great ability with accuracy
and did every trick right.

He could land a big amount of punches
with speed and effectiveness to beat you.
He retired as a world champion,
That's something not many guys can do.

Tribute to Horacio Accavallo

The Wild Bull of the Pampas   May 2019

He had technique below the average
you can expect from a big man,
he could knock an opponent out
with a single punch thrown by either hand.
Known as "The Wild Bull of the Pampas",
he faced other giants of his class.
Once they felt his power, they realized he was
one of the greatest punchers there ever was.

He's remembered for his famous fight
against the man known as "The Manassa Mauler".
It was of the greatest fights ever:
Puncher vs Puncher.
He was closed to winning the world heavyweight title.
He knocked the champion out of the ring,
after being knocked down several times.
Despite his effort, he failed to get the win.

Another non-champion from Argentina,
besides being known as a puncher during his career,
he was the first known boxing figure from his country,
becoming a great pioneer.
One of the greatest punchers ever,
he could easily knock someone to the canvas.
That was the opponent's fate after getting hit
by the Wild Bull of the Pampas.

Tribute to Luis Ángel Firpo

El Látigo   May 2019
("The Whip")

One of Argentina's greats, he was known
as "El Látigo", or The Whip.
He was a fighter some guys
would've preferred
not to even deal with.

He was a southpaw who was ready
and could hit with both hands.
Not only in Argentina,
but also in Europe, he earned many fans.

In three occasions, he won
the super lightweight championship of the world.
If he lost the title, he always recovered it,
becoming one of the great fighters in the sport.

He was determined fighter with a power left hand.
He gave Argentina a lot of glory.
He was one of Argentina's best fighters ever
and one of the best super lightweights in history.

Tribute to Juan Martín Coggi

He destroyed every rival he faced
in his long reign as a super flyweight.
He was known as "The Thai Tyson", since he did
the same thing like the great heavyweight.
Like many competitors in the lighter weights,
he didn't have a big frame,
but his devastating punching power
made him of the biggest punchers n the game.

He suffered only one defeat
when his pro career being.
But then, kept winning fight after fight
and he never lost again.
A southpaw with a powerful left hand,
he knocked down his opponents with regularity.
If he was knocked won, he got up
to knock out his opponents with great facility.

The Thai Tyson never lost as a champion,
having one of the longest reigns in the world,
leaving boxing as one of the greatest punchers ever and
one of the greatest Asian fighters in the history of the sport.

Tribute to Khaosai Galaxy

One of Mexico's all-time greats,
he won world title in four weight-classes.
He had sensational wins as he beat his rivals,
turning in little masses.
One of the best out of Tijuana,
he was one of those fighters like by the crowd
because he gave very good fights.
he made millions of his countrymen proud.

Once his opponents felt his Terribleña,
a very famous combination,
along other punches he threw, they fell apart.
He was one of the greats of his generation.
During his career, he won world championships
from super bantamweight to super lightweight.
Known as "El Terrible", he could give
a great fight any hour of the day.

Like many other great champions, he kept
fighting when he was past his prime.
Nevertheless, he was one of Mexico's best fighters ever
and one of the greatest of all times.

Tribute to Erik Morales

He was a very limited fighter,
but he never gave up.
He was one of those guys who showed guts
when it was time to step up.
This man from Santa Fe
didn't have power in his hands,
but his great determination led him
to give fights that could entertain the fans.

Despite several losses, he showed courage
to win the welterweight championship of the world,
in fight that became one of the biggest upsets
in the history of the sport.
His reign ended after one title defense,
but he left boxing with a memory
of a guy who beat the odds
and one of the biggest Cinderella stories in history.

Tribute to Carlos Baldomir

He could hit hard with both hands
and was one of the great heavyweights in the game.
He was one of the best boxers and one
of the best athletes in the history of Ukraine.
Like his brother, also a world champion,
he was a physical specimen
who was very tall and technical
and could easily beat any man.

He was a fighter that kept his pace in the fight
and fought with intelligence.
He beat his opponents with cleverness and hit them,
so hard that most of them didn't go the distance.
Known as "Dr. Ironfist",
he was one of the best heavyweights in recent memory.
A three-time world heavyweight champion, this legend was
one of the best European fighters in boxing history.

Tribute to Vitali Klitschko

Dr. Steelhammer   May 2019

Like his older brother,
he was also a gifted specimen.
He was also a world champion and one
of the best boxers in the history of Ukraine.
Like his recognized brother,
he won the heavyweight championship of the world
and when had his time, he was
the most dominant champion in the sport.

Known as "Dr. Steelhammer", he had
a great jab and a powerful right hand.
He could knock out his rivals easily
and his boxing technique was elegant.
He had great agility and mobility,
something rare to see in fighters his size.
With his intelligence, great footwork,
he could dominate other guys.

A very dedicated and disciplined boxer,
he was the most dominant heavyweight in recent memory.
A former undisputed world heavyweight champion, he was
one of the greatest in history.

Tribute to Wladimir Klitschko

Many contenders and some guys
that reigned in the heavyweight division
remember this man whose extremely hard punches
could send anyone to his demolition.

He had astonishing power in both hands,
power that could frighten any heavyweight.
His punches were so hard he knock anyone out
any given hour of the day.

He would always stalk his opponents, looking
to land punches wherever he could hit.
His power made him one of those guys
it was hard to go the distance with.

Known as "The Black Destroyer", he never won
the heavyweight champion of the world.
But during his career, he was one of the most
devastating hitters in the history of the sport.

Tribute to Earnie Shavers

The Real Deal   May 2019

Known as "The Real Deal", he's remembered most
for his time as a heavyweight,
although before that, he was the undisputed
world champion as a cruiserweight.
One of the most persistent and courageous fighters ever,
he fought with more heart than a lion.
He showed unmeasurable determination when fought,
becoming the only four-time world heavyweight champion.

He was a fighter with the whole package: punching power,
technique, stamina, heart, and speed.
One of the most determined boxers in history,
he had un unmeasurable refusal to quit.
He is known for his two memorable wins
against the man known as Iron Mike.
He never feared any man and was willing
to face the best every night.

Although like many world champions,
he kept fighting when he was past his prime,
he'll be remembered as one of the best heavyweights ever
and one of the greatest fighters of all times.

Tribute to Evander Holyfield

El Huracán   May 2019
(The Hurricane)

He had his best and longest reign
when he fought as a flyweight.
He's a southpaw with great technique
can show it every day.

He has a very good defense
and shows his technique effectively.
He attacks with great combinations
and hits quickly.

He was also fortunate to reign as world champion
in the super flyweight division.
He's another Argentina's greats and one
of the great little men of his generation.

Known as "El Huracán", or The Hurricane,
he gave Argentina some moments of glory.
He's one of the great little men
in recent memory.

Tribute to Omar Narváez

Another of Argentina's champions,
his technique was admirable.
He was compared to his idol,
the legend known as The Untouchable.

He fought most of his career
in the super flyweight division.
He was of great technical boxers
and stylists of his generation.

He was a great technician
who fought with creativity.
He knew how to maintain the distance,
winning rounds decisively.

It's shame he had a short reign
as the super flyweight champion of the world.
Anyways, he had a very good career
and left his mark in the sport.

Tribute to Gustavo Ballas

He was another Argentinian popular figure.
He took The Greatest to the distance.
He dared to face him and gave him chance, like he did
with other, although his technique didn't have elegance.
He didn't win the world heavyweight championship,
but he was a known contender and fighter
who fought the best of his division
and showed his heart and toughness like a great battler.

A slugger with no finesse,
he was a very charismatic personality
in the heavyweight division, and he imposed
his bravery with tenacity.
Known as "Ringo", his life ended abruptly.
He has to be taken into consideration
because he belonged to a golden chapter of Argentina.
He was one of the great non-champions of his generation.

Tribute to Oscar Bonavena

Goyo   May 2019

He was another heavyweight
who never won the championship of the world.
He challenged for the light heavyweight crown
but was unsuccessful, something that happens in the sport.
He didn't have an exciting style,
but dared to fight any man.
Seeing him fight was like writing a sonnet,
since his style was elegant.

Known as "Goyo", he even dared to face
the greatest puncher in the game.
He fought the best abroad and something lost
in a sport where there's a lot of pain.
Another of Argentina's great fighters,
he was an idol of his generation.
He was a great stylist with technique
fans had to take into consideration.

Tribute to Gregorio Peralta

Hurricane   May 2019
(Middleweight from the 1960s)

One of the great contenders,
he known as "Hurricane",
this great middleweight fighter
was one of great hitters in the game.

Every punch and attack he perpetuated
proved his fists were powerful.
He didn't win the world middleweight title,
although he challenged once and was unsuccessful.

It's a shame his career was cut short
and a wrong and false imprisonment,
a clear proof that he was
a victim of a system.

Despite that, his fights were worth seeing,
leaving fans of his time with a memory
of one of the greatest middleweight contenders
and one of the greatest hitters in boxing history.

Tribute to Rubin Carter

Known as TNT in his career,
he won world title in two weight divisions.
He had an incredible hand speed
that could dazzle millions.

He just needed a fraction of a second
to throw an unexpected combination.
He hit opponents with punches they couldn't see,
becoming one of the fastest fighters of his generation.

Everyone remembers his historic bout with J.C.,
one of the best fighters and hardest punchers in the game.
He was stopped there were two second left in the fight,
and after that, he was never the same.

A fighter with heart that came to fight
and had his moments of glory.
He left fans with a good memory of one
of the quickest and best combination-punchers in history.

Tribute to Meldrick Taylor

He was another known Argentinian figure.
Known as "Martillo" or Hammer,
he was a good middleweight contender
whose punches could drop any fighter.
He could finish any opponent.
One of the hard punchers in the sport,
wherever he hit his opponents, the other guys
felt his punches and it hurt.

He faced the then-champion known as Marvelous
for the world middleweight title.
He knocked him down, but ended up losing.
Nevertheless, his effort was remarkable.
He challenged twice more for a title
and was unsuccessful when he was in his prime.
He still left the sport of boxing
as one of the greatest punchers of his time.

Tribute to Juan Domingo Roldán

He was one of Mexico's great champions
and of the all-time greatest bantamweights.
His opponents couldn't avoid his power
even if they tried in many ways.
His left hook and right hand were
his best weapons in the ring.
Every time he hit his opponents,
he got a quick win.

Known as "Cañas", this knockout artist was one
of the most frightening punchers in the sport.
His fists led him to a long reign
as the bantamweight champion of the world.
And although he challenged unsuccessfully
for the world super bantamweight title
and his bantamweight reign came to and,
his career was remarkable.

He was a great champion that gave
his country a lot of glory.
He was of Mexico's greatest fighter, one of the greatest
punchers, and one of the best fighters in history.

Tribute to Carlos Zárate

He was one of those fighters who progressed
as time passed.
He was another of Mexico's great champions
and one of the greatest punchers there ever was.

His punching power, especially his left hook,
had a lot of explosiveness.
His opponents fell to the canvas hard
once he hit them with effectiveness.

His knockout wins were proof of why
he was one of the greatest punchers in the game.
His punching power and quickness led him
to a long world welterweight championship reign.

Although he lost his title to a young cobra and had
other losses, he left fans with a memory
of one Mexico's greatest fighters
and one of the greatest punchers in history.

Tribute to Pipino Cuevas

His hands didn't have a lot of power,
but he fought with the heart of a stallion.
His temperamental style led him to become
a world super bantamweight champion.

Palma was another of Argentina's great champions.
His frontal style could drive any rival insane.
He was fighter people like to watch
even after his title reign.

Many people who watched him
remember his fighting days.
Palma left the sport as one
of the Argentinian greats.

Tribute to Sergio Víctor Palma

He was known as "Hurricane Hank",
among other nicknames he had in his career.
He was a fighter whose fights
you couldn't miss any month of the year.
He threw and land, threw and landed
punches until the end of every round.
He applied suffocating pressure
until knocking his opponent down.

He measured every second of the clock with each punch,
imposing his will on his rival, putting him through pain.
It was like a locomotive who wanted
to run faster than another train.
It was that suffocating style of volume-punching
that got him the job done.
He did that every time he stepped on a ring
and usually won.

He had outstanding achievements
when he imposed his will constantly.
He's the only boxer to hold
three world championships simultaneously.
There's not enough words to describe this legend
who was great to watch when he shined.
He left the fans of his time a great memory
of one of the best boxers of all times.

Tribute to Henry Armstrong

Big Daddy   May 2019

Known as "Big Daddy", he was a giant
who impacted the heavyweight division.
He was a fighter
that was a fighting attraction.

He could move well in the ring,
had stamina, and beat other guys.
He was great at the in-fighting,
something rare to see in a fighter his size.

He won the world heavyweight title twice
and lost only once when his career shined.
He fought enough to leave fans with a memory
of one of the great heavyweight fighters of his time.

Tribute to Riddick Bowe

He was known as "The Lion".
Originally from England,
he had amazing ring skills
for a big man.
He was a brilliant heavyweight
who used his jab effectively.
Once he hit his opponents with the right hand
or another punch, they fell thunderously.

It was very rare to see
a fighter with a tremendous physique
with that kind of mobility
and a good technique.
A big, strong fighter who knew how to use his reach,
he was a three-time heavyweight champion of the world.
He lost it twice and regained it twice,
proving why he was The Lion.

He made several title defenses in his reigns
when he had his glory.
He was one of the best heavyweights ever
and one of the best fighters in history.

Tribute to Lennox Lewis

One of boxing's great stories,
the fighter known as "The Cinderella Man",
overcame the odds
in a way that could amaze any boxing fan.

In a period of time where many people
struggled during the Great Depression,
he beat the odds to become a world champion
in a historic fight where he showed his determination.

He was a big underdog when he challenged
for the heavyweight championship of the world.
But he didn't give up and won
the biggest title in the sport.

Although his reign didn't last a lost,
left fans with a great memory
of an example of heart and perseverance
and his win of one of the biggest upsets in boxing history.

Tribute to James J. Braddock

Known as "Cyclone", this fighter
had two reigns as a middleweight.
He was a slugger who always came to fight
and was one of the best of his day.
He attacked his opponents with no clemency
and even though his style lacked finesse,
it had an effective offense, worked for him
and was able to beat the best.

He had a very famous rivalry
with man known as Sugar Ray,
the best pound-per-pound fighter of all times,
and the best of his day.
He had four good fights with him,
able to beat him twice,
an achievement that couldn't be done
by other guys.

One of those fighters who should be remembered,
he was stopped only once as a professional,
which means he could take a good punch.
His wins were always sensational,
leaving boxing who watched his fights
during the 1950s with a very good memory
of one of the greatest middleweights of his time
and one of the best fighters in history.

Tribute to Gene Fullmer

Known as "The Executioner", he was a world
champion for a long time as a middleweight,
after he lost that championship,
he had another two reigns as a light heavyweight.
Whatever his fights ended by knockout
or went the distance,
he was a very astute fighter
who fought with a lot of intelligence.

The Executioner had a little bit
of everything in his style of fighting,
something rare to see in every fighter
and it was dazzling.
That crafty, technical, and unpredictable style
led him to a very long middleweight reign.
And despite still fighting at such an old age,
he was one of the smartest boxers in the game.

He had twenty successful title defenses
as the world champion in the middleweight division.
He had two light heavyweight title reigns, becoming
of the most accomplished fighters of his generation.
His career lased almost three decades,
leaving millions of boxing fans with a memory
of one of the best technicians ever
and one of the best boxers in history.

Tribute to Bernard Hopkins

Known as "Macho", he was fighter
opponents always had issues with.
He was extremely elusive in the ring
and had blinding speed.
He attacked with punches someone couldn't see
and fought with aggressiveness.
Even the best fighters in the sport
struggled to deal with his quickness.

An extroverted personality in boxing,
there was of Puerto Rico's best fighters there ever was.
He faced great champions during his career
and he beat them with class.
A three-time champion, he won world championships
from super featherweight to super lightweight.
"It's Macho Time", that the announcer would say
every time he had a fight date.

Although Macho fought when he was past his prime,
he left fans with a memory
of one of Puerto Rico's greatest champions ever
and one of the best boxers in history.

Tribute to Héctor "Macho" Camacho

One of Great Britain's greatest champions,
he had more power than people thought.
Known as "The Dark Destroyer",
he destroyed almost every rival he fought.
He was a fantastic fighter with explosive punching power,
he could knock guys out easily.
He showed no pity to his opponents,
finishing them ferociously.

He had a short world champion reign
as a middleweight.
But had a longer and more known
reign as a super middleweight.
He attacked with powerful bombs
from all angles making the fans pay attention.
A guy with power, ferocity, and speed, he was
one of the greatest punchers of his generation.

His career lasted a decade,
leaving fans and experts with a memory
of one of the greatest punchers of all times
and one of the best European fighters in history.

Tribute to Nigel Benn

El Tyson de Abasto   May 2019
("The Tyson of Abasto")

He was known as "The Tyson of Abasto",
a well-deserved nickname.
His rivals felt to the canvas quickly after feeling
his punching power that could also cause pain.

He fought in a another country to win
the world cruiserweight title.
He became another of Argentina's world champions,
which was remarkable.

He retired and then, came back to become once again
the cruiserweight champion of the world.
Although he lost it after one title defense
and retired again, he left his mark in the sport.

Tribute to Víctor Emilio Ramírez

Known as "Lita" in his career,
who felt the abysmal punching power
of this light heavyweight from Argentina
felt to the canvas harder and faster than a flower.

A puncher with power in both hands,
he had a short career in the sport,
but it was enough for him to win
the light heavyweight championship of the world.

When he won, he gave his people of Santa Fe
and the whole country of Argentina a moment of glory.
And even though he lost it in his first defense
and retired, his name will remain forever in history.

Tribute to Miguel Ángel Cuello

Known as "Uby", he had great tactic
and used his left hand perfectly.
A very good technical boxer,
he could give a boxing lesion wonderfully.

With an accurate attack, he beat a tough guy
to win the super lightweight championship of the world
and become a part of the list
of Argentina's world champion in the history of the sport.

Although he lost the title in his first defense,
his ring skills were terrific.
Originally from Mar del Plata, he was one
of those technicians who could easily give a boxing clinic.

Tribute to Ubaldo Néstor Sacco

He wasn't a tremendous puncher,
but he was a great stylist in the sport.
Corro was another Argentinian fighter who won
the middleweight championship of the world.

Coming from a good Mendoza boxing school,
he was a good counterpuncher and had great timing.
Opponents struggled a lot
when they to deal with his style of fighting.

The pugilistic atmosphere will remember Corro
as a stylist who could win.
He was a wonderful technician
who performed very well in the ring.

Tribute to Hugo Pastor Corro

The Little Bull of Mataderos   May 2019

Known as "The Little Bull of Mataderos",
his style was a fan favorite.
One of Argentina's first figures in boxing,
he was always ready to bring it.

He had a temperamental style, going forward
and attacking, always imposing his courage.
He could've become a world lightweight champion,
but a serious illness took his life at a young age.

It was a sad loss for Argentina that faced
the abrupt end of this great lightweight.
The Little Bull of Mataderos had more bravery
than most fighters show today.

Tribute to Justo Suárez

He was a great fighter who had
first reign as a super featherweight.
Known as "Thunder", he was one
of the most exciting warriors of the modern day.
He also won a world title in the super lightweight division,
where he also had a good reign.
He always showed a mentality of iron
was one of the greatest action fighters in the game.

One time, he was about to lose the world title
was seeing with only one eye.
Then, knocked his opponent out with a left hook
in an exciting fight.
Known also as "The Blood and Guts Warrior",
he could give hard punches and take them in the ring.
He would take a lot of punishment to land
his barrage of punches to win.

There was no reason to miss his fights.
Those who watched Thunder have a memory
of witnessing some historic fights of this man,
who was one of the most exciting action fighters in history.

Tribute to Arturo Gatti

He was another one of Mexico's great fighters
and of the best little men of his day.
He had very explosive and great punching power
for a light flyweight.

He fought on the orthodox stance,
but could fight both positions.
He could fight as a southpaw too
as he landed hard and quick combinations.

Known as "Chiquita", no one
could get cocky with him in the ring.
He could knock some out
with a great punch to get a win.

He had three reigns was a light weight
and several title defenses in his time of glory.
He was one of Mexico's best fighters ever
and one of the best in history.

Tribute to Humberto González

Zamora was another knockout artist
in the bantamweight division who could annihilate anyone.
Once he hit his opponents a couple of times
with his fists, they were gone.

He was a world bantamweight champion
and one of the greatest punchers in the game.
He destroyed every challenger he faced
during his reign.

Although he retired young,
he had his moments of glory.
He was another one of Mexico's world champions
and one of the greatest punchers in history.

Tribute to Alfonso Zamora

He had a very particular style
with his guard always very low.
But once he hit his opponents with a solid punch,
they were ready to go.
Known was "Prince", he had
a very long reign as a featherweight.
He was one of the best featherweights and one
of the best British fighters of his day.

He was brilliant fighter
who always made an extravagant entrance.
He was great with gloves on and could hit do hard
most of his opponents didn't go the distance.
He suffered only one defeat
in his entire career as a professional.
His reign as the featherweight champion
of the world was sensational.
This fighter nicknamed Prince
was a great one to watch in his prime.
He was one of Great Britain's greatest fighters
and one of the best boxers of all time.

Tribute to Naseem Hamed

El Maestro   May 2019

He's another member of the long list
of Mexico's all-time greats.
He had a great fighting style
and was among the best flyweights.

He didn't have punching power,
since most of his fights went the distance.
But he had great tactic,
and he fought and attacked with elegance.

Known as "El Maestro", when he entered the ring,
his rival was always bigger and he was smaller.
But he was tough and had great heart
like the typical Mexican fighter.

He worked with an aggressive volume of punches
during his long reign as the flyweight champion of world.
He was one of the greatest Mexican fighters ever
and one of the best boxers in the history of the sport.

Tribute to Miguel Canto

Manitas de Piedra   May 2019
("Little Hands of Stone")

He had similar nickname
to the great Panamanian legend.
This boxer was also one of boxing's
greatest little men.

He had great punching power in both hands
for a light flyweight.
A fighter with good technique, he was
one of the best light flyweights of his day.

He had four reigns as a light flyweight,
always being a great fight attraction.
Every time he fought in a ring,
the fans were entertained with action.

For a fighter in the lighter weights,
he was a big attraction and had a lot of glory.
He was one of the best light flyweights ever
and one of the best boxers in history.

Tribute to Michael Carbajal

He was one of Cuba's great fighters.
He was known as "El Feo", or the Ugly One.
His boxing style was a good example
of how to get the job done.
Although he could hit hard,
he moved around the ring like a kangaroo
and was very elusive.
If you wanted to box, he could out-box you.

He had a very short reign
as the welterweight champion of the world.
But he was one of the best
technical fighters in the sport.
A smooth boxer who had very good defense
and used lateral movements fluidly,
he was a very difficult target to hit
and he threw combinations quickly.

He fought from the welterweight
to the middleweight divisions, leaving fans with a memory
of one of the best Cuban fighters ever
and one of the best boxers in history.

Tribute to Luis Manuel Rodríguez

Another one of Mexico's great champions,
he wasn't nicknamed "The Mouse" for any motive.
He was a southpaw with fascinating technique
and his jab was effective.

He was a technical fighter with accuracy,
but if he had to fight,
he would do it to get his rival's attention
and make it an exciting night.

He showed his ring skills in different countries.
He had a reign as a bantamweight,
but he was luckier and had three reigns
as a super bantamweight.

Although he lost the last fight of his career,
he'll be remembered as a warrior with class,
one of Mexico's best fighters,
and one of the best boxers there ever was.

Tribute to Daniel Zaragoza

Known as "El Maromero", he was
another Mexican great and was charismatic.
He was a man who came to fight
and he was fantastic.

He did an acrobatic move every once in a while
when he fought in the ring.
He excited the crowd with his performance,
even more when he got a win.

Besides daring a fight, he could elude and avoid
his rival's punches, driving him insane.
An extroverted style with charisma and greatness,
he had a world featherweight title reign.

He was a charismatic and entertaining fighter
who was exciting to watch in his prime.
He was one of Mexico's greatest fighters ever
and one of the greatest of all times.

Tribute to Jorge Páez

A very well-conditioned fighter,
he was a great super lightweight.
Known as "Thunder from Under", he was
a disciplined fighter in every way.

Coming from a very good Soviet boxing school,
his fighting technique was sensational.
He was one of Russia's great champions
who achieved success as a professional.

A very dedicated fighter,
he had punching power in both hands,
especially in his right hand, great reflexes
and a technique that could impress many fans.

His talent led to two reigns
as the super lightweight champion of the world.
He was one of the greatest punchers and one of the best
super lightweights in the history of the sport.

Tribute to Kostya Tszyu

The great Román   May 2019

He was a magnificent technician
who could also hit with both hands.
Not even the best lyrical poet could describe
this boxer who was another one of Mexico's great champs.

The great Roman fought
in many places of the world
to prove why he was one
of the best super flyweights in the sport.

He was a two-time world super flyweight champion,
defending it in many occasions.
The fans who witnessed his greatness
during his career were millions.

An accident ended his life abruptly,
a sad ending for this glory
who was one of Mexico's greatest fighters
and one of the best boxers in history.

Tribute to Gilberto Román

The Golden Rooster   May 2019
("Galo de Ouro")

Nicknamed "The Golden Rooster", he was
the best fighter in the history of Brazil.
His punches could have the impact
of a missile.
Besides being known for being
greatly skilled on defense,
he had great tactics and threw a variety
of combinations to prove he had great offense.

He first won the world bantamweight title,
defending it against any men,
then lost it against a great fighter from Japan,
the only one to beat this Brazilian legend.
He retired and then, made an outstanding comeback,
winning the featherweight championship of the world
to show why he was Brazil's best fighter ever
and one of the best in the history of the sport.

Tribute to Eder Jofre

Chapo   May 2019

He always got the knockout win
with a lot of facility.
He put almost every rival away early
easily, besides showing his quickness and agility.

With great ring movements
and a right hand that was pure dynamite,
the man known as "Chapo" could make sure
his opponent had a short night.

His right hand was a powerful weapon,
but he also had plenty of power in his left hand.
He made his opponent struggle
and his punches entertained every fan.

He was a three-time world lightweight
and a super lightweight champion in his time of glory.
He was one of the greatest punchers ever
and one of the greatest fighters in history.

Tribute to Edwin "Chapo" Rosario

Like many Mexican fighters,
he made his pro debut when he was a teenage boy,
but he let his fists do the talking
and gave his fellow countrymen a lot of joy.
Known as the "Baby-Faced Assassin",
he was the typical Mexican fighter
who was willing to engage in an action fight,
showing he was a great battler.

One of the great Mexican idols, he won
five titles in three weight divisions.
The fans who watched him fight
during his remarkable career were millions.
He was also a great technical boxer
who had wins of great importance.
His fights excited the crowd, whether they
ended by knockout or went the distance.

He had lot of guts and could finish a fight like a cobra
in a career where he truly shined.
He was one of Mexico's greatest fighters ever
and one of the best of all times.

Tribute to Marco Antonio Barrera

One of Panama's best boxers ever,
he had a great reputation as a stylist.
Known as "Bujía" in his career,
when it came to technique, he was an artist.

All he did in the ring
was prepare his motors perfectly,
so his fists and ring movements
could perform wonderfully.

A great technician with great defense and reflexes,
he dodged millions of punches during his day.
His crafty style led him to two reigns
as a light flyweight and as a flyweight.

A great ring and technical magician,
he was magnificent boxer to watch in his prime.
He was one of the best light flyweights ever
and one of the best boxers of all times.

Tribute to Hilario Zapata

Kid Pambelé   May 2019

One of Colombia's greats, known as Kid Pambelé,
his fights were more entertaining than a Cumbia dance.
He had good power in both hands,
although many opponents went the distance.

A very good technical boxer,
he had the technique of an artisan.
His superb qualities in the ring
helped him deal with any man.

Kid Pambelé had two reigns
as the super lightweight champion of the world.
He fought in many places and was one
of the best in the sport.

He had a technique many wished they had.
He gave Colombia many moments of glory.
He was one of the best super lightweights ever
and one of the best fighters in history.

Tribute to Antonio Cervantes

Paret   May 2019

Paret was a boxer with good movement
and was very good fundamentally.
He didn't have a big punch, but he moved
and threw punches quickly.

He could take a punch and was one
of those entertaining fighters in the sport.
He had two short reigns
as the welterweight champion of the world.

He lost his life in his last pro fight
after many battles in his career.
Everything ended in the third fight of a trilogy
in what became a sad event of that year.

Tribute to Benny Kid Paret

He is a member in the list of Puerto Rico's champion
in the history of that island.
His humility and ring skills
were something appreciated by every fan.

A fighter with good punch and a technique
that not every guy has in the sport,
he gave Puerto Rico glory when he won
the light heavyweight championship of the world.

Known as Chegui, this legend
was great to watch when he had his time.
He was one of those battlers
worth seeing during his prime.

Tribute to José Torres

Rocky   May 2019
(From Colombia)

Known as Rocky during his career,
he was a guy who came to fight.
Regardless of the punishment he took,
he gave fans a lot of excitement in a night.

He was a very hard hitter with both fists.
Whether it was his left or hand,
whenever he landed a good punch,
he could hurt any man.

This legend fought everyone,
making his fellow countrymen proud.
This man, who fought in the middleweight division,
always did a good bout.

His great talent led him
to the middleweight championship of the world.
He was one of the greatest punchers of all times
and one of the best fighters in the history of the sport.

Tribute to Rodrigo Valdez

One of Wales's best fighters, he always
showed his caliber when he stepped on a ring.
There's only thing he did
during his entire career: win.
He was a very talented southpaw
who threw a high punching volume every round.
He also hit hard with both hands
and easily drop an opponent to the ground.

A very unpredictable fighter,
the opponent never knew what he was going to do.
A great in the super middleweight division,
he could overwhelm guys with his speed too.
Known as "The Pride of Wales",
he was great to watch every year.
He became one of the few fighters
to retire without a loss his entire career.

One of the best European fighters
and one of the best southpaws of his generation,
he executed his fight plan
and attacked his opponents with precision.
He had a long and successful reign
as the super middleweight champion of the world.
Then, he beat two legends as a light heavyweight to end
his career as one of the best boxers in the history of the sport.

Tribute to Joe Calzaghe

One of the greatest little men ever
and one of the best in the light flyweight division.
He put his opponents through a struggle
once he started to unload his ammunition.
Like the legend known as "The Korean Hawk",
his famous fellow countryman,
he attacked like a human windmill,
suffocating any rival and frustrating his fight plan.

Known as "Sonagi", dealing with his high volume
of punches was like dealing with his flood.
He threw, threw, and landed punches
wherever he could.
This small ring technician was able to have
seventeen successful title defenses in his reign
as the world light flyweight champion, becoming
one of the longest reigning champions in the game.

He lost and the title, but was able to recover it to become
once again the light flyweight champion of the world.
He was one of the best light flyweights
and one of the best boxers in the history of the sport.

Tribute to Myung Woo-Yuh

The Hawk   May 2019
(The Middleweight)

He was one of those guys someone
sometimes preferred not to share a ring with.
In many occasions, it took him only one punch
to put his opponents to sleep.
He was known as "The Hawk", like the legend
in the super lightweight division.
He faced who could take a punch and was able
to send to the ground.

One of the most terrifying and greatest
punchers of his day,
he put guys away early and easily when he fought
as a super welterweight and as a middleweight.
As a super welterweight and as a middleweight,
he had three reigns as the champion of the world,
leaving the fans with a memory of one
of the hardest punchers in the history of the sport.

Tribute to Julian Jackson

One of the hardest punchers ever,
with his power and amazing strength,
this heavyweight sometimes needed one punch
to defeat a man.

With a thunderous left hook
that take anyone's head off,
he could knock any man down easily
and have a win by knock out.

Known as "The Duke", he was one
of my most frightening punchers in the game.
He was able to win the world heavyweight title,
although he had a short reign.

Although he retired and came back years later,
he still showed his power to the world,
leaving his mark in boxing as one
of the greatest punchers in the history of the sport.

Tribute to Tommy Morrison

One of the best Puerto Rican fighters
in the long history of the ring,
he fought in many places in the world
to fight and win.
He hit very hard with both hands
and his technique had good quality.
He attacked every opponent
with intelligence and without sensitivity.

His left hook was as strong as a hack,
and he landed it accurately.
His right hand was as powerful as a machete,
making his rival feel and fall to the canvas badly.
He was one of the best road warriors
and great champions of his day,
winning world title as a bantamweight,
super bantamweight, and featherweight.

After losing his pro debut,
the man known as "Wii" had an incredible progress,
having a sensational career
and proved his caliber against the best.
Despite some losses, he still showed his greatness
in a sport of skills, heart, and sportsmanship.
One of the best ever, someone can see Wii's fights
and say: "That's how you win a championship".

Tribute to Wilfredo Vázquez

Known as "Sweet Pea", he was awesome stylist,
one any expert would've been delighted with.
With the moves of a basketball player, he was
an expert of hitting and not getting hit.
Any boxing fan who remembers
this legend in a ring
enjoyed this man's moves to dodge punches
on his way to get a win.

He used multidimensional moves
and threw combinations with infinite speed.
He avoided punched with amazing lateral movements
and great moves to avoid getting hit.
He was a victim of controversial decisions losses
that infuriated millions.
But he still managed to become a world champion
in four weight divisions.

He was one of the greats of his generation,
leaving fans and experts with a memory
of one of the best defensive fighters ever
and one of the best boxers in history.

Tribute to Pernell Whitaker

One of the best middleweights ever,
a fighter with a solid jaw and well-trained,
he showed why he was one of the best in his division
and one of the hardest hitters in the game.

He was a southpaw with power in both hands.
He attacked his opponents without any compassion.
He could adapt to his opponent's style,
regardless of the situation.

He threw every punch to his rival's humanity
and landed it effectively.
His opponents fell to the canvas
once they were hit solidly.

He beat one challenger after another during his reign,
annihilating the opposition.
He didn't show any respect to his rivals,
sending them to their demolition.

Only one man went the distance during his reign
as the undisputed middleweight champion of the world.
He lost it in his last fight and then, retired with a legacy
as one of the best boxers in the history of the sport.

Tribute to Marvelous Marvin Hagler

Sugar Ray   May 2019
(Modern times)

At the Olympics Games in Montreal,
he won an Olympic gold medal,
proof that since his amateur career,
he was phenomenal.
He was known as "Sugar Ray", like the original
who's the best boxer ever in the history of the sport.
He had an admirable and charismatic personality
that captivated the world.

He was an extremely smart fighter
that could dictate the pace of the wonderfully.
He could give his opponents a lot of issues
and controlled the tempo of the ring easily.
He threw punches in bunches
with blinding speed.
He could play mental games with his rival
and at the same time, being a difficult target to hit.

He did great feints, avoid punches, and land
multidimensional combinations.
He won world championships
in five different weight divisions.
Although he had a couple of retirements,
Sugar Ray, at his prime,
was a great boxer to watch
and one of the best boxers of all times.

Tribute to Sugar Ray Leonard

Known as Will o' the Wisp,
his defensive skills were superlative.
He was one of the great masters of defense
and his extremely elusive.
One second you saw, the other you didn't.
He moved with a lot of agility
and could avoid and dodge punches
with a lot of musicality.

He managed to avoid hundreds
and hundreds of punches in a day.
In a fight, he went an entire round
without throwing a punch, and won anyway.
He wasn't a big puncher, but other guys
couldn't hit him, no matter how hard they tried.
He could block and avoid punches using his elbows
and his great leg games in a night.

One of the best featherweights ever, he had to good reigns
as the featherweight champion of the world.
He fought for more than two decades, showing why
he was one of the greatest boxers in the history of the sport.

Tribute to Willie Pep

Boom Boom   May 2019

Known as "Boom Boom", this middleweight
was another of the world champions from England.
A southpaw with good technique and good power,
he was willing to fight any man.

Despite his tendency to cuts, he met the
best opponents in the sport
and achieved his dream of becoming
the middleweight champion of the world.

He was a good fighter who could cause
any opponent from the southpaw stance.
He was someone who found a way to win
and his fights brought excitement to fans.

Tribute to Alan Minter

Known as "Phantom", he's a member
of the list of world champions from Germany.
He had great technique in the ring
and showed it wonderfully.
He didn't have a lot of power,
but he could box with intelligence.
In a career where he retired unbeaten,
most of his fights went the distance.

Although he got some decisions
that weren't like by the fans,
this German fighter had good skills
and could land punches effectively with both hands.
He had twenty-one successful title defenses
as the super middleweight champion of the world,
having one of the longest reigns
in the history of the sport.

Tribute to Sven Ottke

Smokin' Joe was a legendary fighter,
like very few in the heavyweight division.
With a left hook that could break a tank,
he could a rival to his extermination.
He was a machine that always went forward,
attacking his man with relentlessness.
He made his opponent feel his power and always
imposed his determination and aggressiveness.

He beat The Greatest in the famous mecca
of sports in New York.
It was the beginning of a trilogy and on
of the greatest rivalries in the history of the sport.
He was a gladiator that lost only to two
of the greatest fighters in history.
He was one of the best boxers in history.
His fights left fans with a great memory.

Tribute to Joe Frazier

One of France's best fighters ever
and of the greatest of his day.
Known as "The Orchid Man", he fought in almost
every division, from flyweight to heavyweight.
Besides punching power, he was really skilled
and smart for a man of his size.
He was one of the best Europe had ever seen
and skill could beat bigger guys.

He debuted as a pro when he was a teenager,
but he was willing to fight any man.
As he moved up in weight, he beat opponents
with skills and powerful punches thrown by either hand.
His style looked someone who practiced savate,
but it helped him to show his ability.
He had great speed and could put guys away
with his powerful punches landed with facility.

The Orchid Man was able to win
the light heavyweight championship of the world.
He was one of the best European boxers ever
and one of the best in the history of the sport.

Tribute to Georges Carpentier

Big George   May 2019

People could notice when he entered the ring,
his instinct was intimidating.
The way he pulverized his opponents
with the mentality of an exterminator was amazing.
Every time he fought with the gloves on,
he imposed his punching power and strength.
He had equal demolition power in both hands
and could easily stop any man.

Even after his first retirement,
which lasted a decade, he made a comeback,
and proved he still had his power
and could put any rival away when he attacked.
Known as "Big George", his first reign
was one of terror and demolition.
His second reign was one of a personality
that was more liked by fans of his generation.

Big George had two reigns
as the heavyweight champion of the world.
He was one of the greatest punchers ever
and one of the best fighters in the history of the sport.

Tribute to George Foreman

He was known as "The Motor City Cobra"
and also nicknamed "The Hitman".
He was a tall and extraordinary fighter who could hit
hard with both hands, especially his right hand.
He was tall, lanky, well-trained, and
with the physical appearance of a basketball player.
But once his opponents felt his power in their jaw,
they even had to forget about saying a prayer.

His talent as a fighter led him to win
world championships in five weight divisions,
becoming a multiple-time champion and one
of the most accomplished fighters of his generation.
He knew how to use his reach to his advantage,
could box very well, leaving fans with a good memory
of one of the greatest punchers of all times
and one of the best boxers in history.

Tribute to Thomas Hearns

Salazar didn't have knockout power
and a great technical skill.
But he had an indomitable fighting spirit
and did great fights imposing his will.

We can say that during his career,
he was a fighter of that class.
This fighter from Chaco fought like the great
Argentinian champion he really was.

He was unlucky in his title shots, but he didn't give up
and became a champion of the world
in the flyweight and super flyweight divisions to become one
of the greatest Argentinian fighters in the history of the sport.

Tribute to Carlos Gabriel Salazar

One of the best heavyweights ever, he
was one of the greatest of his generation.
He had more twenty successful title defenses
during his reign in the heavyweight division.
Known as "The Easton Assassin",
he could the jab tirelessly
and there were other punches in his arsenal
he could throw and land accurately.

His technique in the ring made him
one of the longest reigning champions in the game.
He beat one challenger after another
during his dominating reign.
A fighter with one of the best jabs in history,
maybe the best jab ever, nobody ended up laughing
after being in the ring with this legend
known as "The Easton Assassin".

Even though he kept fighting
when he was past prime,
he was one of the best heavyweights ever
and one of the best boxers of all times.

Tribute to Larry Holmes

One of the best technicians ever,
he was known as "The Fighting Marine",
a well-deserved nickname he got
for his marvelous style in the ring.
He had a smooth and fluid technique
and made a fight look like a game of chess.
He was a fast and intelligent boxer
who could beat the best.

He was able to beat The Manassa Mauler,
one of the biggest wrecking machines of all times.
He beat him twice when both legends
were in their prime.
He beat him in the first fight
to win the world heavyweight championship
and beat him again in the Long Count fight,
always showing his amazing ring generalship.

A technical fighter who landed lefts and rights precisely,
he retired as the heavyweight champion of the world,
leaving boxing with a legacy
as one of the best boxers in the history of the sport.

Tribute to Gene Tunney

His punching power was clearly noticed
since his days as an amateur.
His punching power in both hands
was something really hard to endure.

He was a fighting machine in the ring.
Kil-Moon had a very short pro career.
But it was good enough to show
that exciting style fans liked to cheer.

One of South Korea's great champions, he had two reigns
as a super flyweight and as a bantamweight,
he beat his opponents quickly,
becoming one of the greatest punchers of his day.

Despite suffering only two defeats, he managed
to become a two-time champion of the world.
He was one of the greatest South Korean fighters
in the history of the sport.

Tribute to Sung Kil-Moon

The Tiger   May 2019
(From Poland)

He was one of Poland's world champions.
Although he had a reign as a cruiserweight,
he was more known for all the title defenses
he had as a light heavyweight.
He could hit hard with both fists.
If he was knocked down,
he managed to get up and make his opponent
stay in the canvas until the referee reached the ten-count.

Known as "The Tiger", he went after his rival
and he attacked relentlessly.
This Polish star hit with solid bombs anywhere
and put guys away mercilessly.
He had twenty-three title defenses during his reign
in the light heavyweight division.
He exterminated most of his challengers
when he unloaded his ammunition.

Although he lost twice at the end of his career,
he reigned as the light heavyweight champion of the world
when he was at his best; he was one of the longest
reigning world champions in the sport.

Tribute to Dariusz Michalczewski

He was unlucky at first chance
of winning a world title.
But in his second shot, he won it
and his reign was remarkable.

He was a southpaw who cut off the ring very well
and his fights were always exciting.
He had a great killer instinct, he moved
and had great in-fighting.

Watanabe was one of the best
super flyweights of his day.
He pressured his opponents with constant combinations
when he fought as a super flyweight.

He suffered only losses in his pro career,
leaving fans with a memory
of one of the best Japanese fighters ever
and one of the best in history.

Tribute to Jiro Watanabe

Saensak   May 2019

He won the super lightweight world title
in his third fight as a professional.
For of the great warriors in the lighter weights,
that achievement was sensational.

Saensak had two reigns as world champions.
One of the world champions from Thailand,
he put his opponents away with solid blows
thrown by either hand.

Although he had a short career,
Saensak was able to make history
by becoming a world champion in his third pro bout,
giving Thailand great moments of glory.

Tribute to Saensak Muangsurin

Irish   May 2019
(The super lightweight)

Known as "Irish", he had a good career
fighting mostly as a super lightweight.
He didn't have the flashiest style, but he was
one of the best action fighters of his day.
He may have several losses in his career,
but he could give hell to any opponent.
And regardless of the number of scheduled rounds,
his fights always had excitement.

He threw every punch with power,
especially his left hook to the liver.
Whatever rival felt it, he ended up
laying in the canvas crying a river.
Everyone remembers fights with the man
known as "Thunder", in a great trilogy
that had action from the first round to the last one
in became three of the best fights in history.

His fights were witnessed and enjoyed
by fans of the whole world.
The man nicknamed "Irish" was one
of the most respected fighters in the sport.

Tribute to "Irish" Micky Ward

Emile   May 2019

It was worth seeing Emile fight
with arena full in capacity.
He was a great who could box
using his speed and ability.
He wasn't known for his power in hands
or being a knockout artist.
But he had the quickness and the technique
of a good stylist.

He was a fast mover and threw quick combinations
and moved smoothly around the ring.
Emile was a boxer who just did enough
to get a win.
His ring quality made him earn opponents' respect
and boxing fans' admiration.
He won world titles from welterweight to middleweight,
always fighting and beating the best opposition.

He was one of the most respected figures in boxing,
especially when he was the champion of the world.
His brilliant career made him earn a legacy
as one of the best boxers in the history of the sport.

Tribute to Emile Griffith

He never won the world heavyweight title, but he fought
in a golden era of the heavyweight division.
Chuvalo was a much-known contender
who fought the best opposition.
His chin was beyond remarkable
because he was never knocked down.
He fought some of the greatest punchers in the sport
and was never sent to the ground.

He was very tough opponent
who tremendous power in both hands.
His ability to take punishment and give it too
was something that amazed the fans.
This Canadian heavyweight fighter was a worthy rival
for anyone, leaving fans with a memory
of one of the toughest guys
and having the best chin in boxing history.

Tribute to George Chuvalo

One of the best middleweights ever,
he was a natural knockout artist
who could put any man away with one punch.
He was even a nightmare to the best stylist.
Those who fought him realized
he could really hit that hard.
Known as "The Rock", he attacked his opponents
with no clemency in the ring, always going forward.

Everyone remembers his fights
with "The Man of Still", a great trilogy
in which each fight ended in a great knockout
and were some of the best fights in history.
He even dropped the original Sugar Ray, the best pound-per-
pound fighter in the history of the sport,
who beat him in their fight
for the middleweight championship of the world.

He won the world middleweight title
in a moment when his career shine.
He was one of the greatest punchers
and one of the greatest fighters of all times.

Tribute to Rocky Graziano

Double M   May 2019

He was a difficult southpaw
who fought in two weight divisions.
His powerful punching power in both hands
was witnessed by millions.
He easily demolished every opponent
he faced as a light heavyweight.
Then, he moved up in weight and also won
as a heavyweight.

Known as "Double M", he always
entered the ring prepared to fight.
Those guys who felt his punching power
ended up having a short night.
He was a light heavyweight and heavyweight world champion.
But he'll be remembered more as a heavyweight
who left fans with a memory of one
of the greatest punchers of his day.

Tribute to Michael Moorer

Originally from Uganda, he was one
of the greatest punchers with gloves on.
Known as "The beast", once he hit his opponents
with powerful punches, they were done.

If he landed a good punch on his rival,
he would send him to the canvas badly.
If the opponent got up, something that barely happened,
he would knock him out clearly.

His constant knockouts made him one
of the most tremendous punchers in the game.
During his career, he had
a world light middleweight championship reign.

Despite having two failed attempts to win
the middleweight championship of the world,
he'll be always remembered as one
of the greatest punchers in the history of the sport.

Tribute to John Mugabi

He was a skilled big man who once was
unsuccessful in his first chance for the heavyweight title.
But he had an achievement
that was beyond remarkable.
Known as "Buster", he was a big underdog in his fight
against the man known as The Baddest Man on the Planet,
whose quick demolition of his opponents
caused a big racket.

He was given no chance, but he beat the odds
to win the heavyweight championship of the world.
He took his aura of invincibility away
the biggest upset in the history of the sport.
His heavyweight title reign didn't last a lot,
but he left fans with that great memory
when he beat the odds in that historic night
and achieved one of the biggest upsets in sports history.

Tribute to James "Buster" Douglas

Boom Boom   May 2019
(From the United States)

We can say he was like a little Graziano
who caused an impact in the lightweight division.
One of the great ring warriors of his time,
his fights were guaranteed action.
Watching him fight was exciting.
He could take a punch to land one.
He was a guy who went forward
and land punches to get the job done.

He was willing to mix it up with his opponent
to landed powerful punches of his own.
One they felt their power in either hand,
they were gone.
Known as "Boom Boom", fans will not forget him:
a fighter with the heart of the lion
whose exciting style led him to become
a world lightweight champion.

Tribute to Ray "Boom Boom" Mancini

One of the best of his generation,
Jones Jr. showed his talent everywhere.
He was so terrifically skilled
that opponents couldn't touch him a hair.
When he stepped in a ring, he was a boxer
his opponents couldn't deal with.
Not even science could explain his athletic ability,
incredible reflexes, and hand speed.

When he was at the prime of his career, he was
the closest thing to untouchable.
The way he could pass round after round
without getting hit was admirable.
He showed his great skills, winning world championships
from middleweight to heavyweight.
Although all his reigns were great, he shined more
when he fought as a light heavyweight.

He could counterpunch, dodge punches easily,
and could land hard punches with both hands.
The way he handled his opponents in the ring
was something that astonished fans.
Even though he kept winning and fighting
when he stopped being in his prime,
he'll be always remembered as one
of the greatest fighters of all times.

Tribute to Roy Jones Jr

Irish (The Heavyweight)   May 2019

He was known as "Irish" in his career;
he fought as a heavyweight.
He was one of the most respected
and known contenders of his day.

He was a heavyweight fighter
with good hand speed and could hit hard.
He could counterattack effectively
and could get is opponents in a war.

He was a skilled guy with heart, who fought the best
the heavyweight division could offer
in the golden era of that division.
He dared to fight anybody, anywhere.

He didn't win the world heavyweight title
when he was in his prime.
But he was a talented individual with great battles
against the best of his time.

Tribute to "Irish" Jerry Quarry

Known as "Zurdo de Oro", this Mexican legend
was one of the best of his day.
Thousands of Mexicans and fans worldwide
liked watching this great featherweight.
A fighter with tremendous punching power,
he threw and landed powerful lefts and rights.
His stamina was also one of his best attributes
he showed in his fights.

He wasn't the fastest, but he showed more tenacity
than a puma, causing excitement in the sport.
He showed his qualities in his reign
as the featherweight champion of the world.
One of the best fighters of a time,
he was a two-time world featherweight champion.
He was one of Mexico's best fighters ever,
he fought with the fury of a lion.

Tribute to Vicente Saldivar

El Alacrán   May 2019
(The Scorpion from Mexico)

One of Mexico's greatest champions,
this little man was admired in his country.
His fights were watched in every house,
every neighborhood, every county.

Known as "El Alacrán", he didn't have the best technique,
but his fighting spirit was formidable.
He fought until the end,
which was something admirable.

He was a world flyweight champion
and defended the title like a beast during his reign.
He fought in many places, solidifying himself
as one of the greatest warriors in the game.

He was one of those brave fighters who showed
his determination every fight during his time of glory.
He was one of Mexico's best fighters
and one of the best in history.

Tribute to Efren "El Alacrán" Torres

Bazooka
(From Mexico)

When many people say the word Bazooka,
they think about the Puerto Rican legend.
But there was also a Mexican champion with that nickname
and his fights excited every fan.
This southpaw fighter came to fight;
he had solid power with both hands
and his formidable warrior spirit earned him a spot
in the list of Mexico's great champs.

A fighter who fought mostly as a super featherweight,
he had two reigns as the champion of the world.
He battled from the first round to the last round, becoming
one of the most exciting warriors in the sport.
He had the mentality of a natural battler
who threw rights and lefts tirelessly every fight.
His willingness and will, like al Mexican fighters have,
made fans have an exciting night.

He was a fighting machine that did extraordinary fights,
leaving fans with a great memory
of one of the best action fighters in boxing
and one of the greatest hitters in the history of the sport.

He looked like a force of nature.
He was like a big specimen.
He didn't the best physique,
but he could finish any man.
Known as "The Ambling Alp", he had
incredibly solid hands and great size.
He didn't have a formidable technique,
but his power overwhelmed other guys.

This giant from Italy caught the attention
of many people who followed and didn't follow the sport.
With his size, power, and strength, he won
the heavyweight championship of the world.
This Italian giant gained fame due to his size and power,
although he wasn't the most talented big man.
It was good enough for him to have
a heavyweight championship reign.

Tribute to Primo Carnera

Although he looked like a natural super welterweight,
he won a world championship as a super middleweight.
His abysmal power in both hands
could knock any man out any given time of the day.

One of South Korea's great champions,
Baek was a tremendous puncher.
One the opponents felt their power,
the fight didn't last longer.

Unlike other fighters who excelled in the lighter weights,
Baek excelled in his division.
He hit his rival wherever he could, hurting him
and sending him to his destruction.

Getting hit by this South Korean fighter
was like getting hit by a train.
His devastating fists made him one
of the greatest punchers in the game.

Tribute to In-Chul Baek

Just like Baek, his South Korean compatriot,
he was a world champion in the super middleweight division.
He did the same thing in that weight class:
Win by way of demolition.

His power in both hands was something
opponents could not underrate.
If they get careless, they ended up
having a short day.

Chong-Pal had equal
and destructive power in both hands.
His quick knockout wins
was something that excited fans.

His punching power was his biggest weapon
as a two-time super middleweight champion of the world.
He was one of South Korea's greatest fighters
and one of the greatest punchers in the history of the sport.

Tribute to Chong-Pal Park

Torito (Little Bull from Venezuela)   May 2019

He was a little man who gave
size advantages due to his small height.
But he had a lot of toughness and
imposed his heart every fight.
When he had a man hurt,
he gave the fight a great definition.
That's something he always did
as he moved up in weight division.

Known as "Torito" or Little Bull,
he knew how to get the job done.
He fought many times outside his native Venezuela
to defend the championships he won.
He was a warrior, who came to fight,
throwing and landing hurtful punches with both hands.
He had a great heart who fought the best
and he was one of the great champs.

A world champion from minimumweight to
super bantamweight who came to fight and to win.
He was one of the best Venezuelan boxers
and one of the best in the history of the ring.

Tribute to Leo Gamez

Hitman   May 2019
(From United Kingdom)

This fighter was a British and idol
and his fights were always an attraction.
Every fan who watched him remember him
as a big puncher and a man of action.

He always pressed forward and attacked
his opponents with powerful blows thrown by either hand.
A warrior who came to fight, that's how we can describe
this magnificent fighter from Manchester, England.

Known as "Hitman", he had only three losses
in his career as a professional.
Yet his journey, as it lasted,
was sensational.

He had very good reign as the super lightweight
and welterweight champion of the world.
He was one of the most exciting and one
of the best British fighters in the history of the sport.

Tribute to Ricky "Hitman" Hatton

He was the first Russian world champion
in the country's history.
Arbachakov had a short career,
but it was good enough to have to glory.

He was a fighter who knew when it was
the right moment to attack.
Once their opponent felt his punches,
they went down or stood back.

He was a boxer who fight
and attack with elegance.
Most of his opponents who got hit
by his punches didn't go the distance.

He had a very good reign
as the flyweight champion of the world.
He suffered only was loss in his career.
He was one of best Russian fighters in the sport.

Tribute to Yuri Arbachakov

After winning gold in the Olympics, he won title
as a super welterweight and as a middleweight.
Nino was one of Italy's great champions
and of the best of his day.
If you wanted see who could fight and box,
you had to see this European great
whose skills in the ring
were impossible to underrate.

He had a pretty technique to admire,
even when his fights went the distance.
He could avoid and land punches
and do lateral movements with intelligence.
He was a wonderful boxer
with magnificent ring generalship.
He was an idol watched by millions who witnessed
how he won every championship.

A legend that fought the best of his generation,
he gave Italy a lot of glory.
He was one of Europe's greatest boxers
and one of the best in history.

Tribute to Nino Benvenuti

Soo-Hwan   May 2019

He had short reigns when he fought
as a bantamweight and as a super bantamweight.
Like the typical South Korean fighter, Soo-Hwan fought
with the mentality of a gladiator when he had a fight date.
Many remember his historic fight in Panama
in his quest for his second world title.
The way he showed his determination
in the ring was remarkable.

His Panamanian rival sent him to the canvas
four times in the second round.
He showed his heart
and got up after every knockdown.
In the third round, he put his rival away
to win the super bantamweight title and shock the world
in what became one of the best comebacks
in the history of the sport.

Tribute to Soo-Hwan Hong

His fists didn't have natural power,
but he was a light flyweight with great quickness.
Known as Yanbarukuina, he had also had tenacity
and stamina for a long fight, which helped him succeed.

Another world champion from Japan,
he had a short career as a professional.
But it was good enough to become a champion
and every fight he had was sensational.

He had a good reign
as the light flyweight champion of the world.
He fought enough to give his country moments of glory
and leave his name in the history of the sport.

Tribute to Katsuo Tokashiki

He had great characteristics in the ring,
even though de didn't very powerful hands.
He showed his bravery when it was time to show guts
and he put on a show for the fans.

Known as "Pigu", he attacked with both hands tenaciously.
He threw good combinations quickly.
His movement was one of his virtues,
as moved around the ring perfectly.

He was unlucky in first title chances, but finally
won the light heavyweight championship of the world
to become another of Argentina's world champions
in the long history of the sport.

Tribute to Hugo "Pigu" Garay

His career was like a little chronicle.
He hit wherever hole was available
to become Sweden's first world champion,
an achievement that will be indelible.

Although he could hit hard with both fists,
his best weapon was his dynamite right hand.
With that powerful hand, the fighter known as "Ingo"
could drop any man.

Although he had a short career,
he gave his country a lot of glory.
He was one of Sweden's best fighters
and one of the greatest punchers in history.

Tribute to Ingemar Johansson

Foster   May 2019
(light heavyweight)

One of the best light heavyweights ever,
Foster was a tall and lanky guy,
but with his punching power, especially his left hook,
he could easily demolish any man in a night.
He had good moments and good fights
when he fought as a heavyweight.
But he could easily handle other guys
when he fought in his natural weight.

His indomitable power in his fists made him
one of the hardest punches in the game.
When he won the world like heavyweight title,
he defended it fourteen times during his reign.
He didn't any opponent sigh once he hit them hard
during his time glory.
He was one of the greatest punchers, best light heavyweights,
and one of the greatest fighters in history.

Tribute to Bob Foster

Chitalada was small as a molecule
like many flyweights.
But his fights could entertain
fans in many ways.

With his good punching power, this Thai fighter
could knock his opponents down notably.
And he could fight a smart bout
while battling effectively.

As had two reigns as world flyweight champion,
showing his skilled hands in his moments of glory.
He was one of the best flyweights of his day
and one of the best Thai boxers in history.

Tribute to Sot Chitalada

One of Africa's best fighters ever,
he had equal scary power in both hands.
He also had a great tactic and a technique
that could impress millions of fans.
When he had the chance to finish the fight,
he didn't take long and did it to win.
Once the sent his opponents to the canvas,
they laid in the ring.

Known as "The Professor", he won world championships
as a featherweight and as a super featherweight.
He fought in many places, proving he dared to
fight anyone, anyplace, any day.
He fought and stopped his rival with precision; he even
impressed the American audience in his time of glory.
He was Ghana's greatest fighter ever
and one of the best in history.

Tribute to Azumah Nelson

Winky   May 2019

Winky was a magnificent southpaw
who had an admirable technique and great offense.
But he looked even better
in the ring with his defense.

With his very closed guard and elbows perfectly in,
he was an extremely hard target to hit.
He could frustrate any opponent and
land his jab and good combinations with good speed.

He reigned twice as world super welterweight champion,
always giving a very good boxing exhibition.
He was one of the best super welterweights
and one of the best fighters of his generation.

Tribute to Ronald "Winky" Wright

He had a temperamental style,
where he landed punches wherever it was possible.
He fought like a determined war horse
and his stamina was remarkable.
A well-trained fighter, he was one of those guys
that was a fighting machine.
He threw punches tirelessly until the fight was stopped
or the last bell sounded; he came to win.

Known as "The Marrickville Mauler", he won
world championships in three weight divisions.
One of Australia's greatest champions,
his fights were witnessed by millions.
A relentless fighter who pressed at a high work-rate,
he fought and beat the best opposition.
He was one of Australia's best fighters ever
and one of the best of his generation.

Tribute to Jeff Fenech

Like many in his country,
he started training in Thai boxing.
But then, he switched to the Western style
and became a great champion in boxing.

He pressured his opponents relentlessly with his power
and was of the good little men of his day.
He became a world champion when he fought
as a light flyweight and as a flyweight.

This Thai fighter hammered down his rivals.
Despite his short career, he fought good opposition.
He was one of the great fighters in the lighter weights
and one of the best Thai fighters of his generation.

Tribute to Muanghai Kittikasem

He was known as "Popo", a nickname not usual
for a guy that destroyed rivals in his division.
One of Brazil's greatest fighters ever,
he demolished his opponents without compassion.
A monstrous knockout machine,
he caused terror when he fought as a super featherweight.
With a well landed punch, he could make sure
his opponent laid in the canvas in any way.

His knockouts could stun a crowd.
He fought as a super featherweight and as a lightweight,
winning world title in those two divisions,
but he was better as a super featherweight.
He had only two losses in his career,
leaving fans with a good memory
of one of Brazil's best fighters
and one of the greatest punchers in history.

Tribute to Acelino Freitas

He had the classic European style
you can see every day.
He had very good counterpunching,
something rarely seen in a heavyweight.

He had intellectual logic
and fought cautiously.
He also had punching power
and it was shown notably.

One of Germany's best boxers ever,
his fighting style was scientific.
His intelligence and technique
in the ring were terrific.

Known as "The Black Uhlan of the Rhine",
he won the heavyweight championship of the world.
He was one of the best heavyweights ever,
and one of the best boxers in the history of the sport.

Tribute to Max Schmeling

Another one of the best ever,
he wasn't a gigantic heavyweight,
but he was one of the most intimidating
and hardest punchers of his day.

He threw and his right hand like a hack
and his hook could hurt any man.
He could break guys' teeth with his jab,
a proof he had frightening power in either hand.

One of the biggest intimidators in boxing,
he could destroy his rival psychologically,
and when he entered the ring,
he shattered them physically.

He won the world heavyweight title and
even though he lost it, he had his glory.
He was one of the greatest punchers of all times
and one of the greatest fighters in history.

Tribute to Sonny Liston

Veeraphol   May 2019

After a good Thai boxing background, he switched to boxing
and won the bantamweight championship of the world
in only his fourth professional fight, one of
the biggest achievements in the history of the sport.

Veeraphol could land punches
with power and effectiveness
whether went the distance or ended by knockout,
his punches caught the fans' awareness.

Even though the stadium was under the sun,
he was a very good boxer to watch in his prime.
He gave Thailand many moments of glory.
He was one of the best Thai fighters of all times.

Tribute to Veeraphol Sahaprom

El Búfalo
("The Buffalo")

Known as "El Búfalo" or The Buffalo,
he was another of Nicaragua's all-time greats.
He had two battles with the legend nicknamed Finito,
two memorable fights in the lighter weights.
He had a temperamental nature
that made him go forward.
A fighter with a tough mentality, he could hurt
his opponents because he could hit really hard.

He was a small man like many fighters in the lighter weights,
but he was man who offered a lot action.
He landed lefts and rights wherever was area was available.
He was one of the best little men of his generation.
He won world championships in the strawweight
and the light flyweight divisions in his time of glory.
He was one of the best strawweights ever
and one of the greatest boxers in history.

Tribute to Rosendo Álvarez

Bad Bennie   May 2019

One of the best middleweight contenders,
he wasn't called Bad Bennie for any motive.
He showed no mercy to his opponents
and his power was destructive.
His punches thrown and landed
any area possible could cause destruction.
He had many losses, but he lost
against the best opposition.

An impressive puncher, he was a guy nobody
could get careless with in the ring.
He was stopped only once in his career,
which proves he had a very solid chin.
Although he never won a world championship
and was unlucky in his title shots, he left fans with a memory
of one of the most respected fighters of his time
and one of the greatest punchers in boxing history.

Tribute to Bennis Briscoe

Known as "Jinx", he was a boxer
with outstanding ring generalship.
One of the best light heavyweights ever,
he also competed as a heavyweight.
Besides punching hard with both fists,
he knew how to use his speed with precision.
He fought with style and finesse,
like very few in his division.

He threw good combinations and knew when
to finish a fight, which was great for a light heavyweight.
He became the undisputed world light heavyweight champion
and then, won a world title as a heavyweight.
Even though he lost the last fight of his career,
he was great to watch in his prime.
During his career, he was one of the best light heavyweights
and one of the greatest boxers of all times.

Tribute to Michael Spinks

El Expreso de Chincha   May 2019
("The Express of Chincha")

Known as "El Expreso de Chincha",
he was the best fighter in Peru.
An idol in his country, some fans who watched him enjoyed
watching the thing he could do.

He didn't hit with too much power,
but he showed guts and intelligence.
He was a good light heavyweight contender to watch
even when his fights lasted the distance.

He toughness and style, and although he never
won a world title in his category,
The Express of Chincha will be remembered
as one of the best South American fighters in history.

Tribute to Mauro Mina

Saad Muhammad   May 2019

One of the best light heavyweights ever,
his fights and knockouts excited the crowd.
The thud of his solid punches
sounded very loud.

He was of those explosive hitters
whose punches could hurt anywhere.
If he sent an opponent to the canvas,
the opponent laid there.

A very determined fighter, he won
the world light heavyweight title.
Several of his fights during his reign
were memorable.

Saad Muhammad's career lasted a long time,
living boxing fans with a memory
of one the best light heavyweights ever
and one of the greatest punchers in history.

Tribute to Matthew Saad Muhammad

Joltin'

Known as "Joltin'", this lanky fighter
was one of the great fighters of his day.
He was an entertaining fighter to watch
when he fought as a bantamweight.

It was worth watching him
on television with regularity
because his counterpunching and busy style
of fighting had high-level quality.

He was very decided to attack and stunned
his rivals with his punches in the ring.
That high-work rate and counterpunching
helped him win.

This fighter from Philadelphia, Pennsylvania
knew all the tricks in his time of glory.
He was one of the best bantamweights ever
and one of the best boxers in history.

Tribute to Jeff Chandler

Tae-Shik   May 2019

This fighter from South Korea
fought mostly as flyweight,
but he had the punching power
of a middleweight.

With his spectacular power, he won
the flyweight championship of the world.
Although he lost it after one title defense, he left
his name in the history of world champions in the sport.

Tribute to Tae-Shik Kim

A fighter from the former Yugoslavia,
he was a good southpaw who could fight.
He had well-schooled technique
fighters don't show every night.
A boxer from a good European boxing school,
Parlov had good speed,
he knew all tricks in boxing
and was a difficult target to hit.

He won the world light heavyweight title
whose reign didn't last long.
Although he had short career, it was successful.
This Croatian genius knew how to get the job done.
A great amateur and a world champion,
Parlov had a lot of glory.
Those fans who watched his fight
ended up with a good memory.

Tribute to Mate Parlov

El Temible   May 2019
("The Fearsome")

He was another Mexican world champion.
Known as "El Temible" or "The Fearsome",
Once his opponents felt his power,
in a couple of rounds, they were gone.
He had incredible stamina, punching power,
and a courage you don't see in may today.
He attacked throwing hard punches with both hands
and he had his best moments as a lightweight.

Everyone remembers his first fight
with the great one nicknamed "Pretty Boy".
He gave him a hard battle and clearly beat him,
but the judges robbed him and stripped him of that joy.
People also remember his first fight with a fighter
known as "Chico", one of the best fights in history.
Even though he lost that fight, he and his opponent
made fans leave the arena with a great memory.

He dared to face anyone and he shined in his reigns
as the lightweight champion of the world.
El Temible was a great battler and was great to see
in the time he lasted in the sport.

Tribute to José Luis Castillo

Another of Cuba's great fighters,
he wasn't a counterpunching stylist,
but his demolishing fists made him
a great knockout artist.

Known as "The Ox", he was one of the most
feared middleweight contenders in the game.
He landed punches and knocked guys out
with lefts and rights that caused equal pain.

Although he never won a world title,
he left many fans and experts with a memory
one of the best Cuban fighters ever
and one of the greatest punchers in history.

Tribute to Florentino Fernández

He was a very tall fighter with incredible stamina
and an amazing work-rate.
He threw a very high volume of punches
when he fought from welterweight to middleweight.
He didn't stop letting his hand go
in any round.
He overwhelmed his opponents
until knocking them down.

Known as "The Punisher", he had two reigns
as the welterweight champion of the world.
His high-rate offense made him
one of the most exciting fighters in the sport.
Although an accident ended his career, he'll
be remembered as one of the exciting fighters of his time.
His time ended prematurely, but he was
a good fighter to watch during his prime.

Tribute to Paul Williams

El Indio de Cuajimalpa   May 2019
("The Cuajimalpa Cricket")

He was known as "El Indio de Cuajimalpa",
or "The Cuajimalpa Cricket".
He was a fighter worth seeing
if you paid a ticket.

He was a fighter with a technique
that sometimes, you don't see
and great power with both hands.
He was skilled and tough in the ring.

He held a world championship as a bantamweight
and as a super bantamweight,
defending them against the best opposition.
He showed why he was a Mexican all-time great.

He faced the legend called Bazooka, and even though
he lost, it was one of the best fights of the century.
He was of Mexico's greatest boxers
and one of the best in history.

Tribute to Lupe Pintor

Deuk-Koo   May 2019

Like fighters from his country,
Deuk-Koo was someone who fought hard.
He showed tremendous determination
and could fight like he was in a war.

In his world title fight, he showed he had heart
and was willing to take a punch to land one.
He never gave up like the classic Korean fighter
and fought with everything he had every round.

Many remember his fight in Nevada for the
lightweight championship of the world.
Although he lost and did not survived, he fought
a great battle that led to changes in the sport.

Tribute to Deuk-Koo Kim

El Matador   May 2019

He had an extroverted personality
and the public noticed it instantly.
But if the opponent got careless with his power,
he could get knocked out quickly.

He didn't have the best technique,
but he always had a puncher's chance.
If his opponents felt his power, there was no way
they could go the distance.

Known as "El Matador", he won world titles
as a welterweight and as a super welterweight
to become another one of Nicaragua's world champions.
He was one of the greatest punchers of his day.

Tribute to Ricardo Mayorga

He was another of Puerto Rico's world champions.
A southpaw who was consistently good,
He could fight a smart fight
and put his opponent away whenever he could.

He lost in his first chance to win
the world welterweight title
against a fellow countryman,
but his next achievement would be remarkable.

In his second title shot against The Punisher,
he was the underdog and the smaller lion.
But he did a great fight and pulled off the upset
to finally become the welterweight world champion.

Although he lost the title in his first defense,
he had a great campaign as a welterweight.
He'll be remembered for his journey and pulling off
one of the biggest upsets of his day.

Tribute to Carlos Quintana

He was known as "El Magnífico",
which means magnificent.
That's what he was in the ring, whether his fights
went the distance or had a short end.

He could throw and land
good and hard combinations with both hands.
Like the classic Mexican fighter, his skill
and will in a fight could entertain millions of fans.

He could take good lefts and rights
to land many of his own.
He could fight intelligently and punch everywhere
and end a fight in any round.

His fights with Rafa were great battles,
each of them guaranteed action in their rivalry.
He had two reigns as a super bantamweight.
He was one of Mexico's best boxers in history.

Tribute to Israel "El Magnífico" Vázquez

He had an electrifying style
and showed it every fight.
The fans were always excited
when they watched him at fight night.
Known as "Mi Vida Loca", he was one
of the most exciting fighters of his generation.
He attacked with both hands quickly
and attacked with precision.

He was also willing to mix it up
when the fight was on.
He gave the fans their money's worth
every minute of every round.
He won several world championships,
from super flyweight to featherweight,
always fighting the best opponents available
and making them struggle in any way.

He fought anyone regardless of size, talent, and variety;
and he was worth watching every year.
His life ended as he was nicknamed
during his great career.

Tribute to Johnny Tapia

El Torbellino   May 2019
("The Whirlwind")

One of Puerto Rico's best boxers, he was
known as "El Torbellino" or "The Whirlwind".
He didn't have a lot of power, but he had
a great style that helped him win.
He didn't always win by knockout,
but he had acceptable defense
and attacked effectively with both hand
to show he had good offense.

He had a very sophisticated technique
worth seeing in the ring.
He fought in many places and gave Puerto Rico
moments of glory with every win.
A quick and tenacious boxer, he had two reigns
as the super featherweight champion of the world.
He was one of the best super featherweights ever
and one of the best boxers in the history of the sport.

Tribute to Samuel Serrano

El Mosquito   May 2019

Known as "El Mosquito", he was
another of Argentina's world champions.
He was short, but he proved fighters
in lighter weights can fight like lions.
Once the bell sounded, he fought
like a human volcanic eruption.
He fought tough, using some tactics
fans can't take in consideration.

He had several title shots and didn't win,
but he competing in the sport,
showing his tough nature and in his sixth title, shot,
he won the light flyweight championship of the world.
Although his reign ended,
he had his moments of glory.
And that night in Mar del Plata, where won the title,
gave many Argentinians a happy memory.

Tributo to Luis Alberto Lazarte

He was known as "El Tigre Colonense",
since he was from Colón,
a city of his country Panama.
He was a pure boxer that could get the job done.
He was technician with great finesse
and was not an easy target to hit.
He used both hands to land punches
and moved with speed.

One of Panama's greatest fighters, he had two reigns
in the lightweight division.
he had wins and losses,
but always against the best opposition.
He was a great strategist who knew the precise moment
to attack and knew when to use either hand.
One of the greatest boxers in the ring ever,
he was a great artisan.

Tribute to Ismael Laguna

Patterson had a little small physique
for someone who fought as a heavyweight,
but he dared to fight
the best men of his day.

He threw combinations with good accuracy
and landed punches with great hand speed.
He had a closed guard, which helped him to block
or avoid punches, proving he was hard to hit.

If he was knocked down several times,
he would always get up
to keep fighting, which it meant
he never gave up.

He had two reigns
as the heavyweight champion of the world.
He was one of the best heavyweights
and biggest gentlemen in the history of the sport.

Tribute to Floyd Patterson

El Relámpago   May 2019
("The Lightning Strike")

He was known as "El Relámpago",
which means the lightning strike.
He came from a good Mendoza boxing school
and he showed it every fight.

He could land any punch hard
and used his hands scientifically.
He knew how to keep his distance
and box efficiently.

He gave Argentina a moment of greatness
when he won the featherweight world title in Hungary.
his technique and great tactic
gave Argentinians a great memory.

Tribute to Julio Pablo Chacón.

He was a fighter with good offensive arsenal
and moved with a lot of quickness.
He threw his combinations with fluidity
combined with affective aggressiveness.

He used his powerful left hook very well
when he threw his combinations every round.
He gave fans a good reason to watch him when he
quickly sent his rivals to the ground.

Known as "Terrible", he could
go the distance with his opponent in a night,
or with some good punches landed,
he could make it a short fight.

He had three reigns
as the super welterweight champion of the world.
He was one of the best super welterweights
and one of the best boxers in the history of the sport.

Tribute to "Terrible" Terry Norris

Chico   May 2019

Known as "Chico", he was a skinny,
lanky fighter with a big height.
But he had an unquestionable heart and great power
and he could give anyone a hard fight.
During his career, he fought
as a super featherweight and as a lightweight.
He had the temper of a warrior and was one
of the most exciting battlers of his day.

Everyone remembers his rivalry with El Temible,
especially the first bout in a memorable night.
He was knocked down twice in the tenth round, but
came back to beat his opponent and win the fight.
That display of courage and determination
was shown before the world.
His life ended abruptly in a sad way, but he was
one of the great warriors in the sport.

Tribute to Diego "Chico" Corrales

This fiery bull from California
imposed his fury and toughness.
He destroyed his opponent without mercy
and with great ruthlessness.

He fought of his pro career
in the light middleweight division.
He was a hard-punching machine
that sent his opponent to his destruction.

Known as "Ferocious", he had two reigns
as the light middleweight champion of the world.
He faced the best opponents in boxing and even though he
didn't always win, he dared to face the best in the sport.

Tribute to Fernando Vargas

Rarely the middleweight division had seen someone
put guys away as easily as the fighter known as G-Man.
One of the most powerful punchers either, he could
knock someone out with one punch thrown by either hand.

It didn't matter if he hit his opponents in the body
or the head; he would easily knock them down.
The opponents accomplished something if they lasted
more than eighty seconds of the first round.

Although his career ended prematurely, he won
the middleweight championship of the world.
He was one of the best knockout artists
and one of the greatest punchers in the history of the sport.

Tribute to Gerald McClellan

Known as "The Lynx of Parla", he
made his opponents go through pain.
He was one of the greatest fighters
in the history of Spain.
He had better times when he fought
in the light middleweight division.
He beat his opponents clearly with his hands, becoming one
of the best light middleweights of his generation.

He fought in the ring
with the mentality of a determined gladiator.
He attacked his opponents with merciless
and hard punches to show his power was superior.
A gutsy and hard-hitting fighter, he reigned as the
light middleweight and middleweight champion of the world.
He was of the best Spanish and European fighters
in the history of the sport.

Tribute to Javier Castillejo

Schoolboy   May 2019
(Super featherweight)

He was known as "Schoolboy"
during his career as a professional.
He didn't have a lot of finesse,
but his punching power was sensational.

He could knock his opponents out
with solid bombs thrown by both hands.
He had some good rivalries and his fights
always entertained fans.

A tough fighter who could give and take great punches
and always had action.
He landed punches wherever he could,
his offensive attack gave fans satisfaction.

He had two reigns as the featherweight
and the super featherweight champion of the world.
He was one of the greatest punchers
and one of the greatest fighters in the history of the sport.

Tribute to Bobby Chacón

He didn't have a very decent technique,
but he could hit powerfully with both hands.
This Mexican fighter could deliver knockouts
that entertained the fans.

Known as Yory Boy, he could take a punch
and would always go forward.
His opponents ended in the canvas
after they were hit really hard.

He had more than one hundred career wins and won
the light middleweight championship of the world.
He was one of the greatest punchers and had one
of the longest careers in the history of the sport.

Tribute to Luis Ramón "Yori Boy" Campas

Ohashi was a capable fighter who could take
and land punches convincingly.
He had good technique and if he went down, he got up
with the mentality of a samurai and fought courageously.

He was another of Japan's world champions
and fought mostly in the minimumweight division.
He had a short career, but always
fought the best opposition.

He was unlucky in his first title shots,
but then, he gave his countrymen a great memory
by winning the world minimumweight title.
He won it twice to have his moments of glory.

Tribute to Hideyuki Ohashi

Known as "Happy", this Colombian boxer
was an amazing stylist.
His technical and fluid finesse we something
that could stun any boxing analyst.

He used his waist and head movement
to avoid punches with agility.
He didn't have great punching power, but had
great lateral movements and moved with facility.

He won the world bantamweight title.
He made a fight look like a craft work.
He was one of Colombia's best boxers ever
and one of the best in the history of the sport.

Tribute to Miguel "Happy" Lora

Bronx   May 2019
(Davey, super welterweight)

Known as "Bronx", this fighter
could catch a fan's attention quickly.
His power in both hands could send
any opponent to the canvas convincingly.

Once the opponent was hit with a solid punch,
he was gone and the fight was stopped.
He was a very good fighter who had
a very quick rise to the top.

In his short career, he won
the super welterweight championship of the world.
His life had an abrupt and sad end, he could've achieved
so much more in the sport.

Tribute to Davey Moore

"Sugar" Shane   May 2019

He was able to win world titles as a lightweight,
as a welterweight, and as a super welterweight.
He could box his opponents and wipe them out
with solid landed punches in any day.
Besides having solid power in both fists,
he had lighting hand speed.
He moved with a fluidity not many have
was a difficult target to hit.

He always had his prey in front of him
and diminished his rival little by little
with his power and quickness until making
lay in the canvas and looking brittle.
He landed punches to the body and the head
with speed, power, and precision.
Regardless of the divisions he fought at,
he always faced the best opposition.

Known as "Sugar", nobody missed his fights and
even though he fought past his prime,
he will always be remembered as one
of the most exciting fighters of his time.

Tribute to Shane Mosley

Baby Jake

He looked like a little bull in miniature
when he fought as a light flyweight and as a flyweight.
But he was tough as nails in the ring
and could anyone a hard battle any given day.
He was always smaller than his opponent,
but he was solid like a tank.
And once the fight started,
he would be in front of his man.

Known as "Baby Jake", he always
attacked constantly with both hands.
One of South Africa's best fighters, his fights
amazed millions of fans.
A determined little man, his short height
didn't stop him from making history
and show his unmeasurable heart
to give South Africa a lot of glory.

He was able to have reigns as the light flyweight
and the flyweight champion of the world.
He was one Africa's best fighters and
the shortest champion in the history of the sport.

Tribute to Jacob Matlala

Known as "Road Warrior", he fought
in many places in the world.
He always proved himself against
the best fighters in the sport.
This Jamaican fighter could take a good punch
and pressured his rivals without recession.
He was a warrior who imposed his will
against great champions of his generation.

He fought from light heavyweight to cruiserweight,
winning a world title as a light heavyweight.
Whether he won or lost,
he faced the best opposition of his day.

Tribute to Glen Johnson

Rafa   May 2019

Like his brother Dinamita,
he was worth watching on television.
Those opponents who felt his power
were sent to their extermination.
He was willing to fight his heart out
like the great Mexican champs.
He could break any opponent in half
with his lethal power in both hands.

He won world titles as a bantamweight
and as a super bantamweight.
Whenever he could, there no opponent
he couldn't annihilate.
Every remember his rivalry with "El Magnífico",
his fellow countryman.
It was a four-fight rivalry where fists flied from every angle
and entertained every fan.

Rafa was a knockout artist
who had many moments of glory.
He was one of the most exciting fighters
and one of the best champions in Mexico's history.

Tribute to Rafael Márquez

He fought the mentality of a warrior.
He knew how to attack with both hands.
He won the world title abroad to become
one of Argentina's champs.

He was someone who hit hard and
was willing to take a risk in the ring.
Known as Pepe, he would keep battling
to do his best and win.

He won the world lightweight title in France
in his best moment of glory.
He didn't have a long reign, but he gave
millions of Argentines a great memory.

Tribute to Raúl "Pepe" Balbi

Another of Mexico's great champions,
he was someone who hit hard.
Known as "El Travieso", he was someone
who always fought with incredible heart.
This fighter form Sinaloa fought like a bull,
attacking with tenacity and decision.
He showed those guts and character
as he moved up in weight division.

He fought with the mentality of a boa,
always throwing tenacious combinations.
He won world championships
in multiple weight divisions.
He brought action in every fight,
always giving fans their money's worth.
He was one of the greatest Mexican fighters
in the history of the sport.

Tribute to Jorge Arce

www.ingramcontent.com/pod-product-compliance
Lightning Source LLC
LaVergne TN
LVHW051553080426
835510LV00020B/2959